2

Girls with Working and Non-working Mothers

(A Comparative Study)

By

Dr. Indu Bansal

CLASSIC PUBLICATIONS
JAIPUR

Girls with Working and Non-working Mothers

(A Comparative Study)

Dr. Indu Bansal

First Published - 1998

ISBN : 81-87068-09-4

Published by :

CLASSIC PUBLICATIONS
260-61, Chaura Rasta, Jaipur-302 003 India

Printed in India at :
Popular Printers, Jaipur

Foreword

Much of good Research work in our country remains unknown as it is not published. Currently the Publishers don't take interest in this venture it does not seem profitable. As a result the academic world is deprived of the benefit that should accrue of the research.

The Vidyapeth has decided that publication of all good research work at the Institute will be its responsibility.

The provision of unassigned grant by the University Grants Commission has helped the Vidyapith considerably in making this resolve of its possible. Classic Publications, Jaipur has extended its help in wide distribution of the published work. The Vidyapith is grateful to the Commission and the Publisher for their help.

Banasthali

Diwakar Shastri
Secretary
Banasthali Vidyapith

Contents

LIST OF TABLES

LIST OF GRAPHS

Chapter - 1

Introduction

THEORETICAL BACKGROUND

In the modern world of science and technology, with ever increasing demands on the human resources, the role of woman has undergone a tremendous change from that of a housewife to a factory worker, teacher, doctor, engineer, scientist and such others. There are nations which have started utilizing women's energies and abilities even in important defence organizations, national laboratories and in space research experiments. Prior to the 1960's, most people frawned on women doing jobs. Specially, the employed mothers were under the pressure to demonstrate to relations and friends that their employment was not having adverse consequences for children. Today, the public opinion has drastically changed. Nowadays, since the cost of living has soared on account of the world wide inflation, and consequently due to the shooting up of the prices, the burden on man, the traditional bread earner of the family, has increased. The maternal employment has come to be regarded as an economic necessity.

As a result, the traditional expectation that women must derive virtually all of her personal satisfaction from home, hearth and children is no longer widely accepted. Women's desire for accomplishment and fulfillment has expanded and work is recognized as a major way in which these needs can be met. As Goldstein stated, while answering and explaining why would they prefer to work, 37% of the educated women mentioned to 'keep busy', 19% to "make use of education", 13% expressed the 'desire for economic independence' and 12% to 'provide service to others", whole 6% work because of interest in particular field or enjoyment of work itself. Consistent With this new positive perspective, research indicates that maternal employment can bring many benefits to women and also to their preschool through adolescent age youngsters.

With the rising trend among urban female population to enter into jobs more and more, a strong controversy is developing among the psychologists, anthropologists and educationists about the care, broughtup, and development of children. Those, who are more conscious of women's responsibility about the home and children, strongly feel that, under environmental conditions where mothers go for jobs, the total development of children is drastically affected in the negative directions, because mothers do not find sufficient time to look after their needs. This group feels that children develop better personalities under conditions where mothers stay at home.

The effect of mother's working may be damaging to children as the children are likely to feel that their mothers are uninvolved or unsupportive to them, and they feel depressed and inadequate (Piolrkowski and stark 1985). Most of the boys and girls prefer their mother's presence when they are in social difficulties (Gardner and Simpson). In addition she is a warm, accepting authority figure to whom her children look for assurance and guidance when problem arises.

Whereas, the others, who believe that women should utilize their talents and energies by taking up jobs and other occupations, feel that much depends on how the things are controlled and managed by both the parents throught a compromise. This groups cites a number of examples supporting their view which advocates that better personalities develop among those children where both the parents are working. This group feels that there is intrinsic motivation among their children which instigates them to achieve comparatively better awards and grades in schools, and to face competitive trends in the society where they live in. According to this group, this further motivates the parents, including working mothers, to educate their children in a much better way. This group also feels that today better and much highly qualified girls in majority are the products of such homes where mothers are nicely educated and are in good jobs. This group feels that the teaching community where both parents are in jobs has contributed a lot specially by giving better education to girls, even in science, technology and medicine. This group also emphasizes that the intrinsic and extrinsic motivation among girls often motivates their parents to manage such education to them before marriage which may ultimately prove beneficial to their daughters even after marriage. Still this group which advocates in favour of maternal employment often advances a view that the developing girls, specially during the stage of puberty, need close supervision and guidance of the mother because during this stage there is evidence that the behavioural characteristics of the "Negative phase of puberty" is more pronounced in the girls than the boys. But, side by side with this, they feel that the employed mothers can manage things nicely here too with the co-operation of the family members. There is accumulating evidence that employed mothers have less traditional views about child rearing (Mc. Cartney 1984), are less anxious about seperating from their children (Hock, Demeis and Mcbridge 1988), are more committed to their careers (Greenberger and Goldberg 1989).

However, even after knowing so much, the keen desire of investigator to know the realities about the effects of maternal employment on the developing personality of children could not be fulfilled, because of the conflicting and two way advocacy. This led the investigator to know a bit more on this topic from the available literature.

Certain views which where collected in this connection have been reported here. Hurlock (1985) mentions that often threats to good parent child relationship are working mothers. When mothers work outside the home the care of the children must be turned over to relatives or caretakers. If the children are happy in the new environment and like their caretakers, mothers resent it. Should children be unhappy, on the other hand, they will resent their mothers not taking care of them and make mothers feeling guilty about neglecting their parental roles.

We all cherish the image of a mother who greats her child's return from school with an envoloping hug and a batch of warm cookies. But nowadays about half of the working mothers spent less time taking care of their children than do mothers who are housewives (Hill and Stafferd, 1978) and they spend less time within calling distance or in the same room but doing something without their children, like ironing, cooking, reading or watching television (Goldberg, 1977). But there is generaly no difference in the amount, of working mothers and non-working mothers spend alone with their children (Goldberg, 1977). Several psychologists have suggested that the time working mothers spend playing and talking with their children is specially intense and they set aside uninterrupted chunks of time to spend with their children (Hoffman, 1980, Pederson, Cain, Zaslow and Anderson, 1988). Working mothers pay more attention and talk more to their young children.

Gold and Andress have expressed the opinion that boys of the middle class working mothers are often affected and they score lower in intelligence and academic achievement than the boys whose mothers do not work. Tangori (1972) has mentioned that the outcomes associated with maternal employment are more favourable for girls. Girls of working mothers more often have higher educational aspirations and at the college level they are more likely to choose non traditional career such as law, medicine and Physics. Moore (1975) said that sons of the middle class unemployed mothers are more dependent, conforming and inhibited in personality than those whose mothers work. On the other hand this shows that sons of the working mothers are independent and uninhibited. Albarez (1985) remarked that the sons of working mothers seemed to be more demanding and noncompliant and displayed inadequate socialization in the early years. Mc Ghee and Bell, (1982) suggested that a job that improves a mother's morale will improve her relationship with her child, and a job that strains her will cut into relationship.

Family socio-economic status may also interact with employment status to affect maternal and child behaviour. Women with less education may have less interesting as well as less lucrative jobs. Women with lower income work out of necessity, and often for longer hours. They are often less able to buy services and labour saving devices that reduce demands on time and energy at home. There is evidence, moreover, that low income women, as a group, experience less role satisfaction and less social support than higher income women (Crocegberg, 1988), and their parenting may be more adversely affected when they are employed as a consequence.

Eaton (1977) wrote that intellectual benefits accrue for low income children whose mothers work and the explanations they have given for this is that additional income reduces stress and leads to improve daily living conditions. Ramchandran has disapproved this ideology that maternal employment affects the relationship with in the family and social adjustment of children.

Promila Kapoor has the view that the working women, under Indian conditions, become so busy in home and outside that they develop irritable nature and sometimes symptoms of maladjustment which ultimately tells upon the personality development of their children.

In communities where few mothers work, as in India, schools are unlikely to cater the needs of working mothers for supervision before and after school activities for their children. As a result, mothers may feel stressed, burdened and guilty, and their children may sense this. There may be negative effect on their children's schoolwork (Hoffman, 1984). Some children worry that their mothers have too much to do, and they long for the times, usually on weekends, when they can have some undivided attention.

How children feel about the mother's working depends partly upon how seriously her working interferes with the pattern of family life, partly upon what their friend's mothers do, partly upon the stereotype they have learned of "mother", and many other factors. When mothers work outside the home, opportunities for social life and recreation with the family are usually limited and each child must assume more home duties than otherwise. If the child is constantly pressed to do things in a business like way, reactions to the mother and her work will be less favourable (Wellston, 1973, Woods, 1972).

Thus the study of the most of the literature on the effects of maternal employment on the child provided two-way opinions and contradictory views. This did not lead to any conclusion and further motivated the investigator to go deep into the researches. But before doing so, the investigator took up a pilot study on the variables of adjustment of children. The conclusion was that the adjustment of children of working and non-working mothers did not differ significantly in cases where mothers took up the teaching profession. But where the mothers took up personal occupations, significant differences were noted in the areas of adjustment. The children with working mothers displayed comparatively poor adjustment in most of the areas. This disclosed another point that the much depends on the type of profession mothers choose as her career

Ultimately, before finalizing the topic and determining the variables of study for research, the investigator made a thorough study of the related researches to know the realities. The review of these related researches has been presented here.

REVIEW OF PREVIOUS RESEARCHES

The past twenty years have been a time of rapid development of research on how maternal employment affects their family relations. Early researches tended to view maternal employment as having monolithic, mostly negative effects. Non-employed mothers were viewed as the norms. It was assumed that employment had a variety of consequences, such as harming marital relations or children's development. Employed women like unemployed women, were expected to cause family problems.

Earlier researches tended to rely on overly simple approaches. Most of the work reviewed has appeared since 1970. To report the briefs:

1. *Ranade and Ramchandran* (1970)[1] Reported that a large majority of employed women (71%) did not point any adverse effect of their employment on their children and family.
2. *Poznanski et all* (1970)[2] On the basis of study concluded that maternal employment has a definitely positive effect on children's cognitive achievement in schools. On the average daughters of all employed mothers achieve more than daughters of unemployed mothers. Sons in lower and middle class families, but not those in professional families develop their cognitive abilities to a greater extent.
3. *Nelson* (1971)[3] studied the personality adjustment among adolescent children with working and non-working mothers and found that the percentage of children that appear to have adjustment problems were the same for both working and non-working mothers.
4. *Singh* (1972)[4] found that out of the total, 25% women expressed full satisfaction with the time they devote to their children, whereas 75% felt that they really could not devote proper attention to their children and home.

5. *Woods* (1972)[5] reported that the children, specially girls displayed a greater feeling of lack of love, understanding and interest in them, if the mothers worked.
6. *Mani Sharma* (1972)[6] Studied the differential personality patterns of the children of working and non-working mothers and found that children beloging to working mothers differ significantly on scholastic achievement as compared to those belonging to non-working mothers.
7 *Walston* (1973)[7] stated that though everything runs machanically where mothers work, but otherwise there are no significant differences in children as regards relationship, confirmity, adjustment to reality and moods, irrespective of the fact whether mothers work full time, part time, or not at all.
8. *Etaugh* (1974)[8] concluded that the incidence of overt rebellion and outbursts were greater among children of working mothers. On the other hand, the girls were sometimes better adjusted in family roles.
9. *Hoffman and Nye* (1974)[9] On the basis of researches stated that the child in a home when mother is employed experience equalitarian parent relationship, more care by people outside the family and more responsibility for household chores than children in other families.
10. *Bacon and Learner* (1975)[10] studied the effects of maternal employment on the development of vocational role perception of females and found that children of employed mothers often have better social and personality adjustments in schools, more egalitarian concepts about sex roles, and less traditional stereotypes than children with mothers who are full time at home.
11. *Essig and Morgan* (1975)[11] on the basis of study concluded that girls whose mothers did not work, were well adjusted in the area of family as compared to girls of working mothers.
12. *Harrell and Ridley* (1975)[12] Concluded that satisfaction with substitute child care was positively related with maternal employment, but not with the quality of mother child interaction.
13. *Query and Kuruvilla* (1975)[13] did not found any significant difference in the performance of the male and female

adolescents whose mothers were not employed, but there was however, a difference between the males and females when the mother worked in a professional occupations, with daughters performing significantly better than sons.

14. *Nanda and Minocha* (1977)[14] studied the social behaviour of children of working and non-working mothers. The study revealed that children of non-working mothers had better social behaviour than children of working mothers. It was also reported that the children of working mothers remain neglected presumably due to relatively lesser attention they get from their mothers. They became less co-operative, sympathetic and showed indifferent social behaviours.

15. *Rallings and Nye* (1978)[15] concluded that children whose mothers work part time are less likely to feel deprived. Children of mothers who have less pleasant jobs, may feel put upon, feel less need to compromise for their absence, and their daughters are more likely to feel some what neglected.

    In general when the mothers work, their children are more likely to approve of mother's working and of a more egalitarian divison of domestic tasks. Both boys and girls with working mothers are more likely than others to view women as competent.

16. *Gold and Andress* (1978)[16] studied the relationship between maternal employment and development of nursery school children and concluded that children with employed mothers who expressed satisfaction in their roles had the most egalitarian sex role concept.

    Boys with employed mothers had more adjustment problems. The longer the mother has been employed the greater the correlation.

17. *Gold and Anderss* (1978)[17] writes that everything in home, where mothers work outside, runs clockwise as if everything is going on mechaically, but on the other hand it develops punctuality, and children learn to do their own jobs in time. Gold also mentioned that much depends on contacts of children in school situations. Good contacts develop in children some-times better social skills even than their parents.

18. *Hoffman* (1979)[18] on the basis of his study reported that majority of children with the working mothers lacked in self reliance, self initiative, social skills and displayed antisocial tendencies.
19. *Juneja Reeta* (1979)[19] stated that children of working mothers are more independent, more adjusted, socialized and well behaved. Working mothers exercise mild discipline techniques.
20. *Matoo B.K.* (1980)[20] studied the social and emotional adjustment of Boys and girls. The study revealed as general intelligence has been found to have a differentiating role in both social and emotional adjustment areas, the adolescents at the lower intelligence level, were the worst adjusted.

    The difference in emotional adjustment of adolescents of three level of SES have been found significant. The emotional adjustment of adolescents of the middle and the lower strata of society is significantly inferior to that of their counterparts of the higher stratum. The two sexes differ in the emotional adjustment. Boys are superior to girls in their emotional adjustment. This may be due to either consititutional or biological difference, or greater sexual restraints on the girls in our society.
21. *Pal Roma and Sharma, Archana* (1981)[21] on the basis of their study concluded that working class families children get sufficient magnitude of encouragement, democracy, acceptance and love from their mothers. Working mothers dominate their children and also have trust in them. Children get rewards from their working mothers.
22. *Tetenbaum, Joby, Jessican and Travis* (1981)[22] studied educator's attitudes towards working mothers and reported that administrators and teachers were found to have significantly less positive attitudes towards working mothers than pupil-personnel workers. With each group, males were least positive. Replication produced similar results.
23. *Hansson and others* (1981)[23] stated that female subjects whose mothers were employed outside the home during the school years (a) had greater tendency to begin sexual relations before age 19 (b) Expressed less concern regarding the risk of unintended pregnancy (c) Scored lower on an objective test of their practical knowledge about contraception.

24. *Rosenthal and David* (1981)[24] studied the impact of maternal employment on self concept, school achievement, vocational development and perception of parents of 7th to 9th grade students. No significant difference was obtained.
25. *Barbara Robb* (1981)[25] compared the sex role perception of children of working and non-working mothers. Full time employment of the mother was associated with less stereotypical perception of sex appropriate domestic activities.
26. *Francine, Mc Ghee and Bel*l (1983)[26] studied the influence of maternal employment on parent-child interaction and stated that (i) mothers exhibited more care taking, quiet play, and speaking whereas fathers exhibited more active play in both the groups. (ii) Parents from single earner families demonstrated more speaking and quiet play than parents from dual earner families, (iii) sons received more attention in families with non employed mothers whereas daughters received more attention with employed mothers. (iv) There was increased negative effect in families experiencing incongruence between parent's attitudes and the mother's employment status.
27. *Trimberger and Maclean*[27] stated that older children,girls and children who stay alone after school feel more negatively affected by their mother's employment than younger children, boys and children who are supervised after school.
28. *Mackinnon, Brody and Zolinda*[28] studied the effect of divorce and maternal employment on the home environment of pre school children. It was observed that the home environment of children from divorced/working homes were found to be less cognitively and socially stimulating than those of married homes. Children from the married/working and divorced/ working homes had slightly less sex typed rooms than did children from married/non-working homes.
29. *Montemayor and Clayton* (1983)[29] on the basis of observations stated that the relationship between maternal employment and adolescent development is enormously complex and no simple generalizations are possible.
30. *Selkow P.* (1984)[30] studied the effect of maternal employment on vocational aspirations and sex roles of kindergarten and first

grade children. Results indicated that children whose mothers were currently employed chose a greater number of occupations and more masculine oriented occupations than did children of non employed mothers. Girls whose mothers had selected non traditional fields also tended to aspire to less sex traditional careers.

31. *Montemayor* (1984)[31] stated that males had more and longer arguments of greater intensity with their mothers and siblings when their mothers worked than when they did not. Female conflict behaviour was unrelated to the work status of the mother. Adolescents spent less time with their parents when their mothers worked,especially when they worked full time, than when they were non employed.
32. *Goldberg and Esterbrooks*[32] studied the effect of early maternal employment on toddlers, mothers and fathers. Maternal employment was not related to toddler's outcomes. It was related to time mothers spent with their children and to some child rearing attitudes and behaviours of fathers and mothers.
33. *Herriett, Hertsgaard and Martin* (1985)[33] found that maternal employment did not significantly affect the children's work contribution at household chores.
34. *Singh A.J.*(1986)[34] studied the security and adjustment among school going children of working and non-working mothers.

    Findings of his study revealed that the males of non working mothers and females of working mothers feel more secured. With regards to adjustment, the males of non-working mothers and females of working mothers are better adjusted to school environment.
35. *Bhardwaj and Bhattacharya* (1986)[35] on the basis of their study concluded (i) The students with unemployed mothers face more problems in the area of physical health and fitness than their counterparts. (ii) The students with employed mothers have been found to have more problems than their counterparts in the area of friendship, sex and marriage.(iii) No significant sex difference were observed in adjustment areas.

36 *G.Vijaylakshmi* (1986)[36] concluded that the relationship between the employment of mother and the perception of sex

roles of the student was also found to be highly significant. Daughters of employed mothers were found to be liberal in their perception of sex roles.

37. *Kala P.S.* (1986)[37] compared the personality development and adjustment of pre-adolescent children of working and non-working women. The major findings were (i) there was no difference between the perceived parent-child relationship between the groups. (ii) The two groups of working and non-working mothers did not differ in perceived parent-parent relationship. (iii) The girls from the working mothers and boys from non-working group showed better adjustment with peers. (iv) There was no significant difference between the general adjustment of children of working and non-working mothers. (v) The boys from the non-working group were better adjusted to teacher than those of the working group. (vi) The girls from the working group were better adjusted at home than those from the non-working group.

38. *Glueek and Glueek* (1987)[38] discovered that emotional conflict were more prevalent in boys whose mothers worked regularly.

39. *Goswami* (1987)[39] studied the problems of working mothers and their impact on their pre school children. The study revealed (i) There was a multidimensional impact on children of working mothers. The most vulnerable section was the unlettered and low-paid working mothers who were as ignorant of the importance of adequate child care as they were unaware of the facilities available. (ii) Their children were brought up amidst poverty and ignorance because even the minimum of the scanty facilities had not filtered down to them. (iii) The lower middle-class, middle class and affluent working mothers were also plagued by anxieties because the facilities available were not at par with the demand. They suffer from tremendous strain because they had to harmonize the two role of mother and worker.

40. *Bal S.* (1988)[40] concluded that adolescents of non-working mothers have higher achievement motivation than the adolescents of working mothers.

41. *Trivedi Sudha* (1988)[41] reported a significant difference in achievement of girls of working and non-working mothers, but it is not significant in case of boys. Mother's education did not effect the achievement of boys and girls.
42. *Bathurst and Belsky* (1988)[42] on the basis of study concluded that children usually hold less rigid views of sex roles when their mothers are employed. In the cognitive domain, daughters of employed mothers also demonstrate equal or greater competence then do peers, although boys particularly, those from middle class families, sometimes appear to experience negative effect of their mother's work status. Younger children of employed women, who are in non maternal care for more than 20 hours a week, are more likely to have insecure attachment relationship with their mothers than those children where women remain at home.
43. *Mody and Murthy* (1988)[43] reported poorer intelligence scores in children of working mothers at the 12 year age level. Children of working mothers were careless in the early years, emotionally slightly unstable, but independent natured at later years, compared to the children of non- working mothers. Poor adjustment was noted in children of working mothers.
44. *Ramchandran C.* (1988)[44] Carried out a study to identify the effects of maternal employment on the socio-emotional and educational development of children. Results indicated that employment of mother did not effect the socio-emotional and educational development of children. The study further indicated that children of working mothers did not differ in any way from children of non-working mothers in terms of their social maturity, manifest anxiety, achievement in language and arithmatic.

45 *Sharma R.* (1989)[45] Compared the children of working and non-working mothers. Results indicated that from the qualitative point of view significant difference at the adjustment level was found in the children of both the groups. The self concept level of children of working mothers was found to be more than that of non-working mothers. The children of working mothers were found to be better in concentration and confidence, whereas children of non-working mothers were found to be more

excited, anxious, tender hearted, sensitive, dependent and more protected.

46. *Galambos Nancy L. and Maggs Jennifer L.* (1990)[46] studied the mother's and adolescent's perspective of mother's work related status by rating their responses in dual earner familes. They found that global stress was related to mother's decreasing acceptance of the child, according to mother and adolescent. Lower maternal acceptance was associated with poor psychological adjustment in adolescents. Mother's work related stress however, was not associated with mother adolescent relation or adolescent adjustment.

47. *Paulson E., Koman III and John* (1990)[47] Studied the parent child relationship and concluded that sons reported greater closeness with father when mothers were employed and daughters reported greater closeness with parents when mothers were not employed or were employed part time. Mothers reported greater closeness to sons when they were employed but reported greater closeness to daughters when they were not employed or employed part time. Fathers reported no diference in closeness to either sons or daughters regardless of maternal employment status.

48. *Malik and Katyal* (1991)[48] studied the frustration of working and non-working mothers and found that daughters of working and non-working mothers differ significantly in their frustration. Daughters of working mothers are more frustrated than daughters of non-working mothers. Further with regards to reaction to frustration, maximum difference was found in the mean scores of aggression of the two groups.

49. *Engle Patrice L.* (1991)[49] found that when poverty and mother's education were controlled for, no effects of maternal employment on children's anthropometric growth pattern were seen. However the percent of family income the mother earned was positively associated with all anthropometric indicators. Children taken care of by preteen siblings had significantly lower weights for heights than those in other situations, even controlling for SES and maternal employment status. These effects were not found in a 36-48 months old sample.

50. *Malik Sunita* (1991)[50] made an attempt to study the development pattern of career orientation among college and University female students of Himachal Pradesh, in relation to their parental education and maternal employment. The results of the study revealed that there was significant development pattern of career orientation among the female students of Himachal Pradesh from college to University level. Also the higher level of parental education of the female students was found to have the tendency to be facilitative in the development of career orientation, specially in case of those having working mothers. Further, the female University students having low parental education and non-working mothers, exhibit higher level of career orientation than their college counterparts.
51. *Jachuack and Mahapatra* (1991)[51] reported a significant effect of maternal employment status on the creative abilities of children. Sex did not effect the creativity.
52. *Baydar Nazli, Brooks Gunn J.* (1991)[52] studied the effects of maternal employment and childcare arrangements on cognitive and behavioural outcomes of preschoolers and reported that employment in the first three years had detrimental effects on the cognitive and behavioural development of all children regardless of gender or poverty status. Infancy care arrangements affected cognitive behavioural outcomes. Grandmother care was the most beneficial arrangement for cognitive development of children in poverty. Regarding behavioural development, mother care was more beneficial for boys and baby sitter care was most beneficial for girls.
53. *Martha J. and Moorehouse* (1991)[53] studied the relationship of maternal employment patterns to mother child activities and school competence of children for 112 first graders.Results suggested that frequent shared activities may compensate for disruptive features of mother's work or may transmit psychological benefits of works to children. They also suggested that family processes differ as a function of work circumustances and that ecologically appropriate models are needed in studies of environmental influences on development.
54. *Daborah Low Vandell and Janaki Ramanan* (1992)[54] found that maternal employment was related to a number of selection

factors. In comparison of mothers who were not employed, employed mothers scored higher on a mental aptitude test and were more highly educated. Both early and recent maternal employment were also associated with measures of the current family functions. There was less poverty and high home environment scores where mothers were employed. Children's maths achievement and reading achievement was positively predicted by early maternal employment.

55. *Middha Monika* (1992)[55] studied the adjustment, modes of frustration and problems of adolescents of working and non-working mothers and concluded that adolescents of working and non-working mothers differ significantly in their emotional adjustment and problems related to health and physical development, home and family.

However the studies mentioned above report very contradictory results. Moreover, it was also noted that the researches have been limited only to very few variables. The investigator could not find out any study where motivational variables, reactions to frustration, personality characteristics have been studied to a satisfactory level.

Most of the studies were carried out either on infants, preschoolers or on adolescents. The investigator could not find out any study available on elementary school children, specially related with pubertal stage of development, which is the most crucial period of life. Nobody has tried to study through planned investigations the impact of mother's employment on the development of personality, which ultimately determines the unique adjustment to society.

As the children attain the age of puberty, some degree of anxiety and the experience of tension is likely to be related to cope with maturational changes and the acquisition of new roles, particularly since there are no clear cut roles about how to progress to adulthood. The extent of anxiety is partly a reflection of children's perception of the balance of stress and support.

Studies so far done on women's employment are based on family relations, childcare arrangements, and problems of employment. No such research could be traced out where an attempt has been made to know the impact of maternal employment on the development of young children, specially at puberty where,mostly the woman is still the centre for household guidance and role model. Females are still socialized to put their own career second to the jobs of their husbands and to the needs of their children. In families with children society still expects women to assume primary responsibility for the care of children.

It would be surprising to see anyone suggest that fathers may be doing much harm to their children by working outside the home. Mother's responsibility for providing a loving, emotionally healthy environment for her children may conflict with career demands.

The views of the girls regarding appropriate sex and vocational, social roles for women are influenced by the kinds of maternal role models to which they are exposed.

This fact motivated the investigator to take up, this research project, with a view to locate and identity very clearly at least some of the factors pointedly which are effected by maternal employment in either directions.

STATEMENT OF THE PROBLEM

The focus on the impact of mother's rathar than father's work on child development seems sensible, given that work pattern of women have changed considerably, and given that mothers traditionally have been assigned the primary responsibility for the care of children.

Puberty itself is a transition time in the parent-child authority relationship as children assume more independence in decision making. One would expect more tensions between parents and children on issues of achievement, responsibility and family welfare. This ultimately determine the amount of motivation and development of personality among children.

It has already been mentioned that hardly any glimpse is available in some researches or studies on the personality traits, anxiety, self concept, maturity,frustration, achievement motivation, and temperament of children of working mothers. These are the variables which should be specially analyzed and understood, if we have to evolve with all seriousness the type of family environment and for guidance of these children specially for girls.

It is therefore, in the light of this need that the problem was set as follows:

"Comparisons Between Girls Residing with Working and Non-working Mothers at the Pre-pubertal and Pubertal Stages of Development".

It was decided to limit the study to girls only, bacause by nature girls are more sensitive. Moreover, under Indian conditions they have to stay at home more and for longer duration daily as compared to boys. On the other hand, an attempt was also made to include such motivational variables and such personality variables for which good standardized tools could be managed.

JUSTIFICATION OF THE STUDY

In the light of the present economic stress, and increased amount of education, it is becoming more and more pressing for the women to take up jobs or occupations.

In view of this concept, it is the confidence of the investigator that, directly or indirectly, this study will bring into light and at the fore-front most of the areas which are affected in either directions by the maternal employment. Experimental work has shown that mental preoccupations cause parents to become more peremtory and less responsive to their children (zurssman 1980). The girls are more sensitive by nature, and this sensitivity is more exposed among these girls when they have to pass from prepubertal to pubertal stage of development. Girls who report more self reliance under normal conditions may be granted even greater independence and may be encouraged to take on a more mature role in the household.

Certain amount of negative effects are likely to be produced among the children if the chief care taker is employed and is absent from home for a major part of the day. The commonly manifested general adverse effects are:

(i) Children do not get full attention

(ii) They lacked regularity in taking food, sleep, entertainment and education.

(iii) The burden of family work increases and they do not get much time to play and other social activities.

(iv) There are also chances of developing antisocial and with-drawing behaviours.

In the case of school age girls dual career couples can not depend on surrogate such as baby sitting or day care personal. Emotional intensity in the family system is at its peak now and often parents specially the mother is the model to her daughter.

This study may disclose how these commonly manifestsed effects are being checked or handled by the working mothers. This study will also tell if the girls really need comparatively more attention of their mothers. On the other hand, this study may also provide or suggest some factors to the school organizers and administrators which should be controlled more effectively in the interest of proper development of children's personality in school atmosphere.

Ultimately, if may lead to all concerned to a more systematic planning of academic, and co-curricular activities in schools, and a more favourable, conducive and healthy environment in homes.

OBJECTIVES OF THE STUDY

1. To make a comparative study of motivational variables viz. Achievement Motivation, Manifest anxiety, Self-concept, and Maturity of the girls residing with the working and non-working mothers at the pre-pubertal and pubertal stages of development.
2. To make a comparative study of some personality variables viz. Traits and Reactions to Frustration of the girls residing with the working and non-working mothers at the pre-pubertal and pubertal stages of development.
3. To locate and identify which of the variables under study are affected significantly and more in either directions by the maternal employment on the onset of puberty.
4. To identify, under which situations, in the light of mother's professions viz, teaching, medical, office jobs and self employment, the girls are more affected by the maternal employment in either directions.

HYPOTHESES

Alternative Form

In connection with this study the following hypotheses have been developed.

1. (Ho) The performance of the girls residing with working mothers and non-working mothers is the same on different motivational variables under study.

   (Hi) The performance of the girls residing with working mothers and non-working mothers is unequal on different motivational variables under study.

2. (Ho) The performance of the girls residing with working mothers and non-working mothers is the same on different personality variables under study.

   (Hi) The performance of the girls residing with working mothers and non-working mothers is unequal on different personality variables under study.

3. (Ho) The onset of puberty does not bring about significant differences in the performance of girls on different variables under study.

   (Hi) The onset of puberty brings about significant differences in the performance of girls on different variables under study.

DELIMITATIONS OF THE STUDY

1. This study will be limited only to girls studying in the secondary and higher secondary schools located within the urban area of Jaipur (Capital of Rajasthan). The city of Jaipur provides numerous opportunities and job preferences for the mothers.
2. This study will not include girls from the rural areas simply because in these areas even under present conditions normally mothers do not go on jobs for one or the other reasons.
3. To make developmental comparisons and to study the effect of puberty on different variables under study, the girls will be selected from two stages of development seperately one pre-pubertal and another pubertal.
4. It has been observed that the equating of the groups under any study gives better results which are more valid, reliable, and dependable. But it is very difficult also to control many variables at a time. So, in this study groups of girls will be equated on the basis of two variables one intelligence and

another SES, because these two affect more the performance of children.

5. As mentioned earlier, under Motivational variables only four will be included in this study viz., Achievement Motivation, Self Concept, Manifest Anxiety, and Maturity.
6. Under Personality variables, only two will be included in this study viz. Traits and Reactions to Frustration.

DEFINITIONS OF TERMS USED

The meaning and definitions of terms used in the body of this research under motivational and personality variable have been given below.

Motivational Variables

The term motivation refers to the causes for initiation, continuation or cessation, and direction of behaviour. The study of motivation is the study of inferred causes for behaviour, because actual causes can not be known with certainty.

Motivational variable under this study are as follows:

Achievement Motivation

A pattern of planning, and of feelings connected with striving to achieve some internalized standard of excellence as contrasted for example with power or friendship. Achievement motivation is determined by a process of decision making, in which an active individual, seeking meaning and control of his or her environment, considers and selects from among the alternative ways of behaviour.

It may be operationally defined as the motive to accomplish something of value or importance, to meet standard of excellence in what one does.

Self Concept

According to B. Kuppuswami (1983)[56] "Self concept means the subjective and reflective representation in consciousness of the individual to himself, including his thoughts, impulses and actions".

James F.T., and Seyown L.E. defined Self concept As "A person's view of himself, the fullest description of himself of which a person is capable of, at any given time".[57]

Operationally it can be defined as the individual's way of looking at himself, and so signifies his way of thinking, feeling and behaving.

Anxiety

It is a reflection of internal tensions or real or imaginative fear of failure. Anxiety involves pervasive apprehension, dread, and a general feeling that all is not well.

Maturity

Intellectual Maturity

Refers to maturity in dealing with intellectual tasks and making decisions and reason out facts. One displays stable interests, desires for explanation of facts, and demands for evidence before acceptance.

Emotional Maturity

Refers to objective interpretations of emotions, constructive display of emotions, and maturity in facing and solving conflicts.

Social Maturity

Refers to maturity in social poise and social tolerance in dealing with individuals and social situations and in the display of feelings of secure acceptance by peers.

Personality Variables

Personality is an individual's enduring persistant response patterns across a variety of situations. It is comprised of relatively stable patterns of action often referred to as traits, dispositional tendencies, motivations, attitudes and beliefs which are combined into a more or less integrated self structure. Personality includes characteristics and attributes that distinguish the individual from others. Here operationally it is defined in terms of Traits identified and referred to by letters of alphabet A through Q4 and Reactions to Frustration.

Factor A

(Sizothymia, A^-vs Affectothymia, A^+). The term affectothymia meaning a tendency to be full of emotional expressiveness, and sizothymia, to describe the flat, dry, highly restrained expressions of the person.

Factor B

(Low intelligence orDull, B^-vs High intelligence or Bright,B^+). The term low intelligence refers to low mental capacity of handling abstract problems and dullness, high intelligence refers to high general mental capacity, insightful fast learning, adoptability and brightness.

Factor C

(Ego weakness, C^-vs Higher Ego Strength, C^+) Ego strength is regarded as a factor expressing the level of natural dynamic integration, emotional control, and stability and also viewed as capacity for frustration tolerance. The C^- individual tends to be easily annoyed, more often dissatisfied, and is discouraged by his inability to meet good standards of behaviour. On the other hand C^+ individual is emotionally mature, calm, stable, faces reality, unruffled.

Factor D

(Phlegmatic temperament, D^-vs Excitability, D^+) This factor refers to the "temperamental" quality of excitability: The D^+ individual reports as excitable, impatient. demanding, overactive and unrestrained, attention getting whereas the D^- is the person who is undemonstrative, deliberate, inactive, complacent and non restless.

Factor E

(Submissive or Obedient, E^- vs Dominance or Ascendence, E^+) This refers to well known factor of ruling and controlling the things. Submissiveness refers to obedience, easily led, accomodating, dependent as contrast to dominance which refers to Assertive, aggressive, competitive, stubborn and hostile behaviour.

Factor F

(Desurgency or Sober, F^-vs Surgency or Enthusiastic, F^+) It represents a relatively fixed trait, of seriousness, caution, and subdueness at the F^- (desurgent) pole and of debonair, happy-go lucky lightheartedness at the surgent pole. Desurgent persons are sober, silent, slow, cautious as compared to surgent persons who are enthusiastic, heedless, talkative, quick and alert.

Factor G

(Low Super ego strength or Expedient, G^-vs Super ego strength or Conscientious, G^+) It depicts the regard for moral standards, the tendency to drive the ego and to restrain the (id) Subjectively the G^+ person views himself as correct in, and a guardian of, manners and morals, persevering, planful, able to concentrate, cautious in thinking before he speaks, responsible, and preferring efficient people to other companions. G^- subjects have lack of acceptance of group moral standards, undependable and disregards obligation to people.

Factor H

(Threctia or Shy, H^-vs Parmia or Venturesome, H^+) The term 'Threctia' for H^- is intended to summarize 'threat' responsiveness, while 'Parmia', at the opposite pole is an abbreviation for "Parasympathetic predominance", i.e., a skinned immunity to threat. The H^- individual reports himself to be intensly shy, slow, and impeded in expressing himself. He dislikes large parties, fearful of situations, easily fearful and distrustful, but very considerate of other's sensitiveness. In the H^+ direction there is a person who is adventuresome, socially bold, active, impulsive, friendly and carefree.

Factor I

(Harria or Toughminded, I^-vs Premsia or Tenderminded, I^+) refers to the temperamental dimension of personality.I+ individuals receive significantly more descriptions as fussing, tenderminded, sensitive, dependent, attention-seeking, anxious about self, slowing-up group performances in arriving at decisions, making social-emotional, negative remarks. I^- at the opposite pole, represents some sort of tough, practical, mature, group-solidarity-generating and realistic temperamental dimension.

Factor J

(Zeppia or Zestful, J^-vs Coasthenia or Circumspect individualism, J^+) In questionnaire responses, the J+ individual prefers to do things on his own, is physically and intellectually fastidious, tends not to forget if he is unfairly treated, internally restrained. J^-refers to the more zestful, vigorous individual who likes group actions, attention, and accepts common standards.

Factor N

(Naivete or Forthright, N^-vs Shrewdness, N^+) It may be refered as socialy acquired pattern of skills or generalized mental alertness. High N refers to such "criteria" as artful, ingenious, flexible in viewpoint, alert to manners, to social obligations and to social reactions to others and shrewd tactical skills. Low N refers to qualities of almost naive emotional genuineness, complete directness, and spontaneous outspokenness having blind trust in human nature.

Factor O

(Untroubled Adequacy or Self assurance, O^-vs Guilt Proneness, O^+) As the questionnaire items show, definite fears, as well as a feeling of inadequacy and lonliness are prominent for O^+ scores. These children are apprehensive, self reproaching, worrying, troubled, depressed and sensitive to people's approval and disapproval. O^- individual are self assured, placid, secure, serene, self confident, cheerful and insensitive to people's approval or disapproval.

Factor Q^3

(Low self-sentiment integration, Q^{3-}vs High strength of self sentiment,Q^{3+}) expresses the degree to which the individual has adopted and invested his interest in an ideal "self regarding sentiment". Low score describes the uncontrolled, careless of social rules, follows own urges which contributes to anxiety. High score is associated with controlled exacting will power, socially precise, compulsive, following self image persons who prove to be.chosen as leaders.

Factor Q^4

(LowErgic tension or Relaxed, Q^{4-}vs High ergic tension or Tense, Q^{4+}) The last of the fourteen factors is referred as pattern of behaviour. Individuals scoring high on Q^4 are described as irrationally worried, tense, irritable, and in turmoil. They are sensitively aware of being criticized by parents for untidiness, phantasy and neglect of good goals. Persons scoring low on Q^4 are relaxed, tranquil, torpid, unfrustrated, composed.

Reactions of Frustration

Obstacle Dominance (OD)

This term refers to a tendency in which the barrier occassioning the frustration stands out in the resposes of the individual.

Ego Defence (ED)

This term refers to the tendency in which the ego of the subject dominates in his resposes while facing the frustrating situations.

Need Persistance (NP)

This term refers to a tendency in which the solution of the frustrating problem is emphasized by the individual in his responses.

Extrapunitiveness (E)

This term refers to a tendency where aggression is turned by the subject on some person or thing in the environment.

Intrapunitiveness (I)

This term refers to a tendency in which aggression is not turned by the subject on some person or thing in the environment, but upon himself.

Impunitiveness (M)

This term refers to a tendency in which aggression is turned by the individual neither on some person or thing in the environment nor upon himself, but aggression evaded in an attempt to gloss over the frustrating situation.

REFERENCE :

1. Ranade, S.N. and Ramchandran, P. *"Women and Employment"* in Pratima Kumari, changing values among young women. New Delhi: Amar Prakashan, 1988, P191.
2. Pozenanski, E., Maxey, A. and Marsden, G. *Clinical Implications of Maternal Employment; A review of research* Journal of American Academy of Child Psychiatry Vol.9, 1970.
3. Nelson Dean, D. *Study of personality Adjustment Among Adolescent children with working and non-working Mothers.* Journal of Educational Research March 1971.
4. Singh, K.P. *Career and Family, Women's Two roles.* Indian Journal of Social Work, 1972, Vol.33, PP115-121.
5. Woods, M.B. *Unsupervised child of the working Mothers.* Developmental Psychology; 6, 1972, P14-25.
6. Sharma, Mani. *Differential Personality Pattern of the children of working and non-working Mothers;* A Ph.D. thesis submitted in Agra University. 1972.
7. Walston, B. *Effects of Maternal Employment On children;* Journal of child Psychology and Applied Disciplines 14, 1973, PP81-95.
8. Etaugh, C. *Effects of Maternal Employment on Children.* A Review of Recent Researches; Merill-Palmer Quarterly, 20, 1974, PP71-98.
9. Hoffman, L.W. and Nye, E. *Working Mothers.* San Francisco: Mossey Bass, 1974, P90.

10. Bacon, C. and Lerner, R.N.*Effects of Maternal Employment on the Development of Vocational Role Perception of Females.* Journal of Genetic Psychology; 126, 1975, PP187-193.
11. Essig and Morgan. *Adjustment of Adolescent daughters of Employed Mothers.* Journal of Educational Psychology; 37, 1975, PP219-223.
12. Harrell, J.E. and Ridley, C.A. *Childcare, Maternal Employment and Quality of Mother child Interaction.* Journal of Marriage and Family; Vol.37, 1975, PP556-564.
13. Query, J.M. and Kuruvilla, T.C. *Male and Female Adjustment on the Sex Role Perception, Interest and Self Esteem in the Kindergarten Girls.* Review of Recent Researches; Vol.11, 1975, P90.
14. Nanda, P. and Manocha, M.K.*Comparative Study of the Social Behaviour of Nine Year old Children of Working and Non-working Mothers.* Indian Journal of Home Science; Vol.11 No.23, 1977, P977.
15. Rallings, E.M. and Nye, F.I. (1978).*Wife, Mother Employment Family and Society, cited in Wesley R. Barr et al; Contemporary Theories About the Family* Vol.I, 1979, P211.
16. Gold, D. and Andress, *D. Relations Between Maternal Employment and Development of Nursery School Children;* Cited by Joyce, Wolfgang, Williams; Middle Childhood Behaviour and Development; New York: Mac Millan Publishing Company. Inc. 1980, P47.
17. Gold, D. and Andress, D. *Developmental Comparisons Between ten Years old Children with Employed and Non-employed Mothers,* Child Development 49, 1988, PP75-84.
18. Hoffman, L.W. *Maternal Employment.* American Psychologist, 34, 1979, P859-865.
19. Juneja, Reeta. *A Comparative Study of Working and Non-working Mothers with Regard to Practices and Problems of Rearing Children.* Indian Psychological Review Vol.18, N0.1-4, 1979, PP20-21.
20. Matoo, B.K. *Social and Emotional Adjustment Patterns of Adolescent Boys and Girls at Various levels of Socio- Economic Status and General Intelligence;* Indian Educational Review; Vol.15 No.1, Jan. 1980, PP110-114.
21. Pal, roma and Sharma, Archana*A Factor Analysis Study of Mother-child Relation Dimension of Working Housewives.* Indian Psychological Review Vol.20, No.2, 1981, PP29-34.
22. Tetenbaum, Joby J., Jessican, Ligher and Mary, Travis.*Educators attitudes Towards Working Mothers.* Journal of Educational Psychology, 1981, 73, PP375-379.
23. Hansson, Roberto, O'Conner, Marry E., Jones warren H. and Blocker J.Jean. *Maternal Employment and Adolescente's Sexual Behaviour*Journal of youth and Adolescence; 1981, 10, PP55-59.
24. Rosenthal and David. (1981).*The impact of Maternal Employment on Children's Perception of Parents and Personal Development;* Child Development Abstracts and Bibliography; 1981, Vol.7, P5-93.
25. Barbara, Robb.*Maternal Employment and Children's Sex Role Perceptions,*Child Development Abstracts and Bibliography;1982, Vol.56, P186.
26. Francine, S.M., Mc Ghee, Paul E. and Bell Nancy J.*Parent child Interaction; The Influence of Maternal Employment;* Child Development Abstracts and Bibliography; 1983, Vol.57, P82.

27. Trimberger Rosemary and MacLean Micheal J.,*Maternal Employment: The Child Perspective;* Journal of marriage and Family, 1982, Vol.44, PP469-475.

28. Mackinnon carol, E., Brody Gene, H. and Zolinda Stoneman*The Effect of Divorce and Maternal Employment on the Home Environment of Perschool Children.* Child Development 1982, 53, P1392-1399.

29. Montemayor Raymond and Clayton Mark, D. *Maternal Employment and Adolescent Develop-ment; Theory into practice* Child Development Abstract and Bibliography 58, No.1-3, PP112-118.

30. Selkow Paula, *Effects of Maternal Employment on Kindergarten and First Grade Children's Vocational Aspirations: Sex Roles;* Child Development 1984, 11, PP677-690.

31. *Montemayor Raymond, Maternal Employment and Adolescent's Relations with Parents, Siblings and Peers;* Journal of Youth and Adolescence 1984, 13, PP543-557.

32. Goldberg Wendy, A. and Easterbrooks, M. (Ann). *Effects of Early Maternal Employment on Toddlers, Mothers and Fathers;*Developmental Psychology; 1985, 21, PP774-783.

33. Harriett Light K.,Hertsgaard D. and Martin Ruth E.*Farm children'sWork in the Family.* Adolescence, 1985, 20,PP 425-432.

34. Singh, Agya Jit. *Security and Adjustment Among School Going Children of Working and Non-working Mothers.* Indian Educational Review; 1986, Vol.21, P47.

35. Bhardwaj, G. and Bhattacharya Rina. *The Effect of Mother's Employment on Adolescent's Problems.* Journal of Education and Psychology; 1986, Vol.43, P186.

36. Vijaylakshmi, G. *A Study of the Relationship Between the Perception of Sex roles and Occupational Choices of Women Students Studying certain Professional and Non-professional Courses;* Indian Dissertation Abstracts; Jan-March 1986, Vol.XV No.1.

37. Kala, P.S. *Personality Development and Adjustment of Preadolescent Children born to Working and Non-working Women From Higher Socio-economic Families,* 1986, Research Centre For Womens Studies, S.N.D.T. University Bombay.

38. Glueek and Glueek, *Working Mothers and Delinquency;* 1987, Child Development 41, p 37.

39. Goswami K.A. *A Study of the Problems of Working Mothers and Their Impact on Their Pre School Children with special Reference to the City of Gauhati.* Thesis for Ph.D. in Education, Gauhati University, 1987.

40. Bal S. *The Effect of Mother's Employment on Achievement Motivation of Adolescents,* Journal of Personality and Clinical Studies; 1988, 4(1), PP81-84.

41. Trivedi, Sudha. *Scholastic Achievement of Adolescent Children of Working and Non-working Mothers.* Indian Educational Review; Vol.XXIII No.3, July 1988, NCERT Delhi PP56-62.

42. Bathurst K. and Belsky K. (1988)*Maternal Employment, Family Environment and Children's Development: Infancy through the School Years* Cited in A.E. Gottfried and A.W. Gottfried (Eds); Maternal Employment and Children's Development; PP11- 58.

43. Mody Sanober N. and Murthy Vinoda N.*The Study of Mental Health of Children of working Mothers.* Journal of Personality and Clinical Studies; 1988, 4(2), PP161-164.

44. Ramachandran. C. *A. Study of the Effect of Maternal Employment on Socio-emotional and Educational Development of children;* in Buch M.B. (Ed.), IV Survey of Research in Education, pp 825-829.

45. Sharma R. *A Comparative Study of the Children of Working and Non-working Mothers;* in Buch M.B.(Ed), II Survey of Research in Education PP892-899.

46. Galambos Nancy L. and Maggs Jennifer L.*Rating Mother's Work related Stress in Perspective: Mother's and Adolescent's in Dual Earner Families.* Journal of Early Adolescente; 1990, 10, PP313-328.

47. Paulson E., Koman II Joseph, J. and Hill John, (P).*Maternal Employment and Parent Child Relations in Families of Seventh Graders.* Journal of Early Adolescence (1990); 10, PP279-295.

48. Malik Archana and Katyal Sudha. *A Comparative Study of Frustration in Daughters of Working and Non-working Mothers.* Asian Journal of Psychology and Educationa; 1991. Vol.24, No.7-8, PP13-17.

49. Engle Patrice L. *Maternal Work and Childcare Strategies in Peri-Urban Guatemala; Nutritional Effects;* Child Development; 1991, 62, PP954-965.

50. Malik Sunita. *Development of career Orientation Among College and University Female Students in relation to Parental Educaton and Maternal Employment: A Cross Sectional Study:* Journal of Education and Psychology; Vol.49 No.1 and 2, April-July, 1991, PP34-39.

51. Jachuak, K. and Mahapatra Sanjukta.*Creativity in Children: Effect of Maternal Employment and Sex;* Praachi Journal of Psycho Cultural Dimensions; Vol.7 No.1, April 1991, PP30-35.

52. Bayder Nazli, Brooks Gunn Jeanne.*Effects of Maternal Employment and Childcare Arrangements on Preschooler's Cognitive and Behavioural Outcomes: Evidence from the Children of the National Longitudinal Survey of Youth;*Developmental Psychology; 1991, Vol.27 No.6, PP932-945.

53. Martha J. and Moorehouse. *Linking maternal Employment Patterns to Mother Child Activities and Children's School Competence;*Developmental Psychology; 1991, Vol.27 No.2, PP295-303.

54. Daborah L. Vandell and Janaki Ramannan.*Effects of Early Maternal Employment on Children from Low Income Families;*Child Development; 1992, 63, PP938-949.

55. Middha Monika. *A Study of Adjustment, Modes of Frustration and Problems of Adolescents of Working and Non-working Mothers* 1992, Unpublished Dissertation Thesis, Banasthali Vidyapith.

56. Kuppuswami, B. *Elements of Social Psychology.* Vikas Publishing House Pvt. Ltd. New Delhi: 1983, PP200.

57. James, F.T. and Seyown, L.E. *Investigation into Self Concept* in Journal of Personality 1959, PP483-498.

Chapter - 2

Method and Techniques

METHOD ADOPTED

This investigation has been planned on the lines of Normative Survey Method of research, which is fact finding with adequate interpretation in the light of the norms. It is essentially a method of quantitative description of the general characteristics of a group. Under this method, the true meaning of the data collected is reported from the point of view of the objectives and the basic assumptions of the project.

The Normative Survey method describes and interprets things as they are. It is concerned with conditions or relationship that exist, opinions that are held, and effects that are evident. It is primarily concerned with present but at the same time takes into consideration the past events and influences as they relate to current conditions. This method deals with the relationships between variables, the testing of the hypotheses and the development of generalizations that have universal validity.

According to Whitney "Normative Survey is an organized attempt to analyze, interpret and report the present status of the social institutions, group or area"[1].

John W. Best opines that this method: "gathers data from a relatively large number of cases at a perticular time. It is concerned with the generalized statistics that result when data are abstracted from a number of individual cases. It is essentially cross sectional"[2].

Some characteristics of normative survey are as follows

(i) It is mostly a cross-sectional type of study but it can also be a Longitudinal one.

(ii) It is not concerned with the characteristics of individuals but with generalized statistics of the whole population or the sample thereof.

(iii) It requires an imaginative planning, a carefull analysis and interpretation and a logical, skillful reporting of the findings.

(iv) It does not aspire to develop an organized body of the scientific laws but provides information useful to the solution of a more fundamental nature.

(v) It may be quantitative or qualitative in the nature.

(vi) Description may be either verbal or expressed.

The techniques which were previously employed to the Normative Survey were observations, questionnaries, rating scales and interview schedules etc. Modern developments in this method have encouraged the application of all types of standardized tools of investigation including even psychological tests and other such instruments which can help in collecting more authentic evidences and informations.

The information reported in the body of this research is mostly of the quantitative type but with qualitative interpretation of the facts.

In the present study, the investigator has used a number of psychological tests and case study for the collection of relevant data as follows :

1. Indian adaptation of R.B. Cattlle's Culture Fair Intelligence Test (Scale 2) used for equating groups on the basis of intelligence.
2. Dr. Gopinath Sharma's Socio-Economic Status Scale to test the SES of the group.
3. Dr. Gopal Rao's Achievement Motivation Test for the study of Achievement Motivation.
4. Dr. Mohsin's Self Concept Inventory for the study of self concept.
5. Dr. Kumar's Maturity scale for the study of intellectual, emotional and social maturity.
6. Indian adaptation of Sarason's General Anxiety Scale for the study of the anxiety.

7. Dr. Cattell's Children's Personality Questionnaire (CPQ) to study 14 traits or factors of personality.
8. Indian adaptation of Rosenzweig's Picture-Frustration Study (Children's form) for the study of the six personality factors.
9. Case study schedule.

The investigator selected these tests for two reasons firstly due to non availability of good tests for use below adolescence, these are sufficiently good tests. Second these tests are valid and reliable to a great extent providing good material for multidimentional depth study, Specially Cattlle's CPQ and Rosenzweig's P.F. study.

DESCRIPTION OF THE TESTS USED

1. CULTURE FAIR INTELLIGENCE TEST:- Scale 2, Form A, Hindi Version (R.B. Cattlle and A.K.S. Cattlle)

This is a non verbal test which requires that the subjects be able to percieve relationship in shapes and figures. It measures intelligence in a manner designed to reduce, as much as possible, the influence of verbal fluency, cultural climate and educational level. This test is adapted to administration either as individual or as a group test.

This test consists of four sub tests (i) Series (ii) Classification (iii) Matrices (iv) Conditions (Topology). It can be used with children as young as eight years and equally appropriately with older children and most adults.

Items and time alloted to each subtest in scale 2 is given below:

TEST		NUMBER OF ITEMS	TIME ALLOTED
Test I	Series	12	3 Mins.
Test II	Classification	14	4 Mins.
Test III	Matrices	12	3 Mins.
Test IV	Conditions	8	2.5 Mins.
TOTAL		**46**	**12.5 Mins.**

In each sub-test some examples are given so that the task requirements and the ways for making their responses on the answer sheet are made clear to the students. In the arrangements of sub- tests a comparativly well known, easy to grasp test has been chosen to start the subject off. In all tests the component items are arranged to occur in order of increasing difficulty. For the administration of the test one has to follow instructions given in the hand book.

The scoring procedure is to give one score for each right item. If more than one answer is marked, no credit is given for that item. The number of correct answers for each of the four tests is recorded in appropriate row in tabular column to obtain the total raw scores. These raw scores can be converted into standard scores for the psychological interpratations. I.Qs can also be estimated with the help of tables in the manual.

The reliability of this test has been evaluated by working out split half, interform correlations corrected to appropriate length, and test retest correlations with the time interval varying from immediate to one week. The co-efficients were 0.76, 0.67 and 0.73 respectively.

The validity was measured by correlating the scale with the pure intelligence factor. For form 'A'it is 0.85, for the sub-test No.I it is 0.76, for sub-test No.II it is 0.54, for sub-test No.III it is 0.76 and for sub-test No.IV it is 0.51. The concrete validity (Correlations with other tests of general intelligence) is 0.70.

2. SOCIO-ECONOMIC STATUS SCALE:- (Dr. Gopinath Sharma)

The present scale was prepared mainly to provide a simple instrument which could be used without spending much time and effort and to obtain a correct measure of socio-economic status of a person. This can be equally used for urban and rural areas.

This tool contains items related to six areas namely parents' education, occupation, monthly income, housing conditions, books and magazines bought in home and household things.

The inventory is self explanatory.The subjects has to read well each item and decide upon any one alternative, from among the alternatives provided after each question, that is best matched with their condition and to indicate it with a right mark in the square provided opposite to that alternative.

The sequence of every item is determined from low to high which shows the number of scores assigned for scoring. Therefore for the first five areas if a subject in a class marked on 5 for education, 3 for occupation, 4 for monthly income, 4 for housing and 3 for magazines and news papers, he will be given 5+3+4+4+3=19 scores for it. For the last area in the scale, i.e. for the household things the items were grouped in to four; namely vehicles, furniture, electronic media material, modern household equipments.The serial number of the alternatives is the scores. The subject has to choose only one alternative from each of the four groups. Thus if a subject marked alternatives numbered 3,3,2 and 2 in the four groups, he will be given 3+3+2+2=10 scores for the last item. This will be added to the previous score i.e. 19 and thus the total scores will be (19+10) 29. Need to give correct responses may be emphasized.

Score range for different SES is:-

1.	1 to 17	Low Socio-Economic status
2.	18 to 37	Middle Socio-Economic status
3.	38 to 51	High Socio-Economic status

.The content validity was established on the basis of opinion of the experts. The reiliability coefficient, calculated for separate components of the scale were as follows:-

Education = .98, Occupation = .93, Income = .93, House = .94, Magazines and News papers = .99, Household things - .84 and for the total test = .97. Due to high correlation found, it was accepted as highly reliable.

3. Achievement Motivation Test :- (Dr. Gopal Rao)

Dr. Rao has developed this test on the lines of Mac Lelland's Achievement motivation test. It is meant for upto Secondry School Children.

There are 20 incomplete sentences, each of which is followed by two possible alternatives A and B, out of which one is an achievement related item. Though both the alternatives are achevement oriented and socially acceptable, yet one of them imply a higher sense of achievement and excellence.

This test may be administered to a group or an individual. It is suitable for use with both sexes. There is no time limit but the group test takes about 8-10 minutes.

The test may be scored with the help of scoring key. For each item, one is high achievement related (HAR) and the other is general achievement related (GAR). The GAR responses get a score of one and HAR responses get a score of three.

The norms are available in the manual in terms of means and standard deviations and in terms of range from low motivated, average and highly motivated subjects.

The reliability of the test was determined by the test- retest method, after an interval of one month. The coefficient of reliability was found to be 0.79.

The Item validity in terms of discrimination value range from 0.25 to above.

4. Self Concept Inventory :- (S.M. Mohsin)

The MSCI includes 48 items consisting of positively or negatively phrased statements about abilities and strengths pertaining to the cognitive, affective and conative areas. The positivly and negatively phrased statements are equally balanced in number, all positively phrased statements affirm a positive quality and all negatively phrased statements deny a negative quality. The acceptance of a statement as characterising oneself signifies, in either case, positive evaluation of the self. The entire inventory is, thus intended to measure variation in self- regard.

The test norms are given in percentiles. Two halves reliability of the MSCI was found to be 0.57 for half and 0.73 for the full inventory, using the SB formula.

For validity, the correlation with Maslow SI test was 0.35 and with MPCI it was 0.40. Both values are significant at less than 0.01 level of confidence. The obtained correlations may be taken as indices of construct validity of the MSCI.

5. Maturity Scale :- (Dr. K. Kumar)

This test measures the level of maturity of the students in three areas-intellectual maturity, emotional maturity and social maturity. The test includes 36 items, twelve for each area. With each item there are four possible responses, outof which the subject has to tick only one response, the weights for different items range from 1 to 4 which refer indirectly to the subject's level of maturity. The item validities of the test range from 0.33 to 0.72 in the terms of bi-serial correlations.

The reliability of the test has been calculated by the test- retest method. The reliability coefficient range from 0.84 to 0.92.

The manual for the scale provides seperate norms for all the three areas of maturity in the terms of means and standard deviations.

6. Sarasons General Anxiety Scale for Children (GASC) Indian Adaptation :- (Dr. A. Kumar)

The scale is helpful to locate the anxiety level of the children upto the age of 17 or 18 years. The scale also categorizes the anxiety level of children into five categories viz: very low, low, average, high and very high.

The scale has been adopted in Hindi language. It has total 45 items related to varied life situations. These items contain an element of anticipation of dangerous and painful consequences. The various situations with which the items are generally related are as follows:-

(a) Health, physical appearence and injury.

(b) Success or failure in his work.

(c) Afraid of animals and strange things.

(d) Social relations and social approvals.

(e) Worries regarding family members and other relatives.

(f) Worries regarding the future happenings.

(g) Afraid of loneliness.

It is a self administering, consumable scale with no time limit. Ordinarily it takes 15 minutes to complete the test. Yes answer to an item means admitting anxiety. Total number of yes answers denotes the raw scores of anxiety.

Coefficient of reliability for the scale was determined by two methods viz split half method and Kuder Richardson formula-20. The reliability is 0.79 and 0.81. The scale is an Indian adaptation of Sarason's GeneralAnxiety Scale for children. Sarason and his associates developed this reliable and valid measure of anxiety while working on a project "Anxiety in school children". They made various predictions emerging out of the theoretical position taken by them and conducted a number of relevant studies to prove those predictions. It can, therefore, be assumed that GASC possesses an adequate 'content' and 'construct' validity.

7. Childrens Personality Questionnaire (The CPQ) form 'A':- (R.B. Cattell)

The present test is primarlly intended for an age range of eight through thirteen. The test is a new aid for the elementry school guidance specialist and for the teacher in the class room. Recent advances based on extensive psychological research have made possible this instrument to give on objective analysis of the individual personality which supplements the teacher's personal evaluation. The CPQ is a standardized test with two forms, A & B, each divided into two parts. Each part can be given in a class period, to a single individual or group.

The CPQ yields a general assesment of personality development, measuring fourteen distinct dimensions or traits of personality which have been found by psychologists to approach the total personality. These different fourteen dimensions are symbolized by letters A, B, C, D, E, F, G, H, I, J, N, O, Q3, Q4.

The table below gives the brief description of these factors.

Table 1 : Primary Source Traits Measured by the CPQ

Low Score Description	Factor	High Score Description
RESERVED, Detached, Critical, Cool, Aloof (Sizothymia)	A	WARMHEARTED, Qutgoing, Easygoing, Participating (Affectothymia, formerly Cyclothymia)
DULL (Crystallized, power measure) (Low intelligence)	B	BRIGHT (Crystallized, power measure) (High intelligence
AFFECTED BY FEELINGS, Emotionally, Less Stable, Easily Upset (Lower ego strength)	C	EMOTIONALLY STABLE, faces Reality, Calm, Mature (Higher ego strength)
PHLEGMATIC, Undemonstrative, Deliberate, Inactive, Stodgy (Phlegmatic temperament)	D	EXCITABLE, Impatient, Demonding, Overactive, Unrestrained (Excitability)

Low Score Description	Factor	High Score Description
OBEDIENT MILD, Accommodating, Easily Led (Submissiveness)	E	DOMINANT, Assertive, Competitive, Aggressive, Stubborn (Dominance)
SOBER, Prudent, Serious, Tacitum (Desurgency)	F	ENTHUSIASTIC, Happy-go-lucky, Heedless (Sugency)
EXPEDIENT, Disregards Rules (Weaker superego strength)	G	CONSCIENTIOUS, Persevering, Staid Rule-bound (Stronger superego strength)
SHY, Threat-sensitive, Diffident, Timid (Threctia)	H	VENTURESOME, Socially Bold, Uninhibited (Parmia)
TOUGH-MINDED, self-reliant, Realistic, No-nonsense (Harria)	I	TENDER-MINDED, sensitive, Over-protected (Premsia)
ZESTFUL, Likes Group Action, Vigorous (Zeppia)	J	CIRCUMSPECT INDIVIDUALISM, Reflective, Internally Restrained (Coasthenia)
FORTHRIGHT, Natural, Artless, Sentimental (Artlessness)	N	SHREWD, Calculating, Artful, (Shrewdness)
SELF-ASSURED, Confident, Secure, Complacent (Untroubled adequacy)	O	GUILT-PRONE, Apprehensive, Worrying, Troubled, Insecure (Guilt proneness)
UNDISCIPLINED SELF-CONFLICT, follows-Own Urges, Careless of Social Rules (Low self-sentiment integration)	Q_3	CONTROLLED, Socially Precise, Following Self-image, Compulsive (High self-concept control
RELAXED, Tranquil, Torpid, Composed, Unfrustrated (Low ergic tension)	Q_4	TENSE, Frustrated, Driven, Overwrought, Fretful (High ergic tension)

Each form is sectioned into two parts (A1 & A2). Each section consisting of seventy statements (total 140).

The test is administered without a time limit, but for younger children it might be better to divide the testing time into two parts, for a given form. A single session should not be expected to exceed fifty minutes. Each statement is followed by two or three alternatives. The subject has to mark his response in one square. The child's answers may be marked directly on the booklet, but for easier scoring a seperate answersheet is available. Since it is recommended that the answersheet always be used when possible, the children should be cautioned to make no mark on the test booklets. The test is administered as per the directions printed at the top of the cover page of the booklet. Scoring is easily and rapidly done by using stencil keys.

Complete instructions for obtaining the raw scores from the answer forms are given on the scoring stencils themselves. Two stencils are required to obtain the 14 scores from each of the test forms.

The reliability calculated as dependability, of each factor on each form is set out in the following table. Since the interval between testing was only two days, any change in the test score must be due basically to unreliability. The next table followed gives homogenity coefficient for each factor. These values were computed using the Kuder Richardsons formula 20.

Table 2 : CPQ Dependability Coefficients : Test-Retest after two Days

(PERSONALITY FACTOR)

	A	B	C	D	E	F	G	H	I	J	N	O	Q_3	Q_4
FORM A	.59	.72	.47	.67	.67	.70	.66	.58	.72	.59	.70	.60	.61	.56
FORM B	.42	.71	.57	.58	.56	.46	.54	.48	.48	.48	.50	.61	.56	.49

Table 3 : CPQ Homogeneities Of Individual Scales

	A	B	C	D	E	F	G	H	I	J	N	O	Q_3	Q_4
FORM A	.51	.37	.67	.58	.53	.60	.59	.52	.68	.25	.40	.45	.55	.41
FORM B	.29	.32	.31	.32	.32	.28	.29	.29	.19	.07	.11	.27	.52	.26

The CPQ is theoretically based; its scales are relevant to the hypothesized structure of personality, and validity indicates both the goodness of the hypotheses and the adequacy of the measure of each hypothesized construct. This is termed concept or 'construct'. Validity (Cattells-1964;Cronbach, 1960). The coefficients for each factor are set out in the following table:

Table 4 CPQ Direct Validity Coefficients

	A	B	C	D	E	F	G	H	I	J	N	O	Q_3	Q_4
FORM A	.55	.82	.73	.83	.33	.91	.72	.64	.69	.65	.52	.68	.79	.76
FORM B	.79	.78	.51	.71	.51	.51	.45	.75	.75	.29	.64	.61	.87	.69

8. ROSENZWEIG PICTURE - FRUSTRATION STUDY CHIL-DREN'S FORM:- INDIAN ADAPTATION (Udai Pareek & Saul Rosenzweig)

The various investigations by Rosenzweig led to a theory of frustration, which formed the basis of exploration in the direction of frustration and reactions. In order to specify his own techniques, he termed it as "Picture Association Study for Assesing Reactions to Frustrations", which was shortened to "Picture Frustration Study" and is now popularly known as P.F. Study. The Rosenzweig P.F. Study may be said to be a controlled projective technique primarily intended to measure reactions to frustrating situations.

The P.F. Study consists of 24 cartoons like drawings, representing frustrating situations. One character in the drawing is shown saying something that causes frustration to the other person dipicted. The subject is required to say or write on the form concerned what the other person would say in that situation. In the children's form the frustrated individual is always the child. Both the forms of P.F. Study can be administered individually as well as in groups.

An effort has been made to include in both forms, the examples from every days life situations.

The Indian adaptation of the children's form of this P.F. Study has been developed by Dr. Udai Pareek. This focused on the developmental pattern of reactions to frustration on Indian children from age 4 to 13.

The reliability and the validity of the Indian adaptation were also determined. The scoring reliability, as found by comparing the scoring by two independent scores, was quite high, the percentage of agreement being 79 with increase to 98 after mutual discussion. Reliability coefficients both for matrix reliability and item reliability were quite high. Stability co- efficient ranged from .51 to .78 and consistency values from 56 to 91.

This study can be administered in about 20 minutes either in group or individually. The subject has to write his responses on the standard examination blank. Instructions for administration are given on the cover page of the test.

It is assumed as a basis for the P.F. Study that the subject unconsciously or consciously identifies himself with the frustrated individual in each pictured situation and projects his own bias in the replies given. This test provides quantitative scores for each Individual. Scores are assigned to each response as to the 'direction of aggression' and 'reaction type'. Under directions are included extrapunitiveness (E)- in which agression is turned into environment; intropunitiveness (I)- in which it is turned by the subject upon himself; and impunitiveness (M)- in which agression is evaded in an attempt to gloss over the frustration. Under 'type of reaction' fall obstacle dominance (OD)- in which the barrier occasioning the frustration stands out in the responses, ego defence (ED)- in which the ego of the subject predominates; and need persistance (NP)- in which the solution of the frustrating problem is emphasized.

From the combination of these six categories there result for each item nine possible scoring factors (and two variants E-I). Scoring is done according to the scoring instructions and scoring samples given in the manual.

This test is generally used to study the dynamic pattern cf child's behaviour.

9. CASE STUDY SCHEDULE

Since it was decided to study some cases out of the sample to know the realities connected with the variables of the study, a case study schedule was prepared on points related with each variable, for example source of achievment motivation, reasons for anxiety and frustration, development of self concept, factors leading to immaturity, and merits and demerits of mother's employment. This schedule was used by the investigator while interviewing and talking to each case.

THE SAMPLE

The sample on this investigation has been selected on the basis of random sampling. In the random sampling the individual observations or individuals are chosen in such a way that each has an equal chance of being selected, and each choice is independent of any other choice.

The concept of randomness has been basic to scientific observation and research. It is based on the assumption that, while individual events can not be predicted with accuracy, aggregate events can. Randomization has two important applications in research:

1. Selecting a group of individuals for observation who are representative of the population about which the researcher wishes to generalize; or
2. Equating experimental and control groups in an experiment. Assigning individuals by random assignment is the best method of providing for their equivalence.

The sample for this research has been selected from primary, secondry and higher secondry schools located within the urban areas of Jaipur in the state of Rajasthan. The sample was selected to be homogeneous in a number of respects- all families were two parent (nuclear), well educated and with first born girls of same average IQ and SES, having only part time maid servent or not at all.

A census of families with working and non-working mothers was conducted through visits to all the schools. The census schedule was designed to collect details on the, name of the child, date of birth, age, class (in which studying), father's name, education and occupation, educational and employment status of mothers, number of siblings, type of family, help available like full time or part time servent.

From this list girls of nuclear families having both the parents, firstborn and age 9, 11 & 13 were selected. The SES scale was administered to all these girls.

On the basis of the scores obtained on the SES scale, practically very few cases were found falling in SES I and SES III. Since the groups were to be equated on the basis of SES also, naturally a need was felt to delete cases with wide variations. So ultimately only those cases were selected for the sample which fell in SES II. This further avoided the problem of equating the groups on this variable.

All these students were administered Cattlle's Culture Fair Intelligence Test and then girls were selected for the sample in various groups on the basis of IQ.

After forming various six groups of girls, it was analysed how far the various groups differ in intelligence and whether various groups of girls have been really equated on the basis of intelligence or not.

The following sample was drawn out randomly for the administration of selected tools:

TABLE-5.

Stage	Age (Years)	Girls residing with working mothers	Girls residing with non-working mothers
Prepubertal	9	50	50
Prepubertal	11	50	50
Pubertal	13	50	50

The following tables present Means and Standard Deviation calculated on the basis of IQ for various groups. Analysis of variance follows:

Table 6 : Means and Standard Deviations based on I.q. for Various Groups

Age groups	Statistics	Girls residing with working mothers	Girls residing with non-working mothers
9	Mean	108.48	109.92
	S.D.	10.55	10.96
11	Mean	110.40	110.26
	S.D.	10.19	12.14
13	Mean	108.98	109.50
	S.D.	9.56	11.56

Table 7 : Analysis of Variance for Various Groups on Intelligence

Source of Variation	df	Sum of squares	Mean square	F
Between Means	5	141.31	28.262	0.24
Within Groups	294	34675.683	117.9445	

The F ratio obtained here is insignificant. This shows that the different means do not differ significantly from each other. This further tells that various groups have been rightly equated on the variable of intelligence.

This helped the investigator to proceed further and so various tests selected were administered on the groups, and thus data were collected.

This sample ultimately came from 40 schools.

For case study 10 students (total 40) were selected from each group. (i.c. 10 girls at prepuberty & 10 at puberty age from those residing with working mothers and those residing with non working mothers).

STATISTICS USED

"Statistics is a body of mathematical techniques or processes for gathering, analyzing and interpreting numerical data. Since the research yields such quantitive data, statistics is a basic tool of measurement, evaluation and research"[3].

There is no doubt that proper use of statistical techniques helps in analyzing and interpreting data in a better way. This gives more correct and best possible information. In most of the cases the statistical techniques of common use do not differ much even if the authors are different. Still, it may be mentioned that practically for all the statistics used here the formulae have been picked up from the book "STATISTICS IN EDUCATION AND PSYCHOLOGY" by H.E. Garrett.

The statistical techniques used in this investigation are the following:

1. MEAN

This statistics has been used in this investigation to study the average performances of the groups of girls on different variables included in this research project. The mean has also helped in obtaining results based on the analysis of variance and t-values.

2. STANDARD DEVIATION

This statistics has been used to know about the spread of the scores around mean on different variables of the study. Further it has also helped alongwith the mean in analysis of varience and in the calculation of t-values.

3. ANALYSIS OF VARIANCE

This statistics has been used to see how far the different groups under this study being six in number differ significantly from each other on each variable included in this study.

4. t Ratio

This statistics has been used to see how far the two means representing the performances of the two concerned groups and connected with the variables differ significantly. It may be mentioned here that the formula used here for calculation of t ratio is that for uncorrelated means.

In addition to this some graphical presentations have been given in the body of this research, these are based on the means of the groups.

REFERENCE :

1. Whitney F.L.; *The Elements of Reasearch,* Bombay, Asia Publishing 1961, P-161.
2. Best J.W.; *Reasearch in Education.* (5th Edn.) N.J. Prentice Hall 1986. PP-80-81.
3. Ibid., p-206.

Chapter - 3

Analysis and Interpretation of Data

This chapter reports all the data collected in connection with this research project. To facilitate analysis and interpretation, the data have been presented in the form of means and standard deviations calculated on the basis of the scores obtained by the different groups of girls at the various stages of development. Since it is comparative study, separate data has been presented for the girls residing with their working mothers and for the girls residing with the non -working mothers. The data in Part A and Part B for each variable under study has been subjected first to analysis of variance, and thereafter t values have been calculated to find out where the groups of girls differ significantly.In cases where F ratio was not found significant, t values were not calculated. The significance level for F ratio was determined at 2.25 for 0.05 level, and at 3.08 for 0.01 level. similarly,the significance level for the t value was determined 1.98 for 0.05 level and at 2.63 for 0.01 level.

It may be mentioned here that in the light of the objectives of the study mentioned in chapter I, this chapter has presented material first for the Motivational variables and thereafter for the Personality Variables. Since this chapter also includes study of variables as affected by mothers profession, and also some case studies, the parts of this chapter have been named as follows:

Part A - Study of Motivational Variables.

Part B - Study of Personality Variables.

Part C - Variables as affected by Mothers professions.

Part D - Case Study.

PART - A

STUDY OF MOTIVATIONAL VARIABLES

It may be recalled here that under "Motivational Variables" only Four variables have been selected for the study. These are Achievement Motivation, Manifest Anxiety, Self Concept, and Maturity. As mentioned in chapter II, these variables were studied with the help of psychological tests. The description of the psychological tests has been given in chapter II. The data for all these four variables has been presented here in this very order, followed by its analysis and interpretation.

1. ACHIEVEMENT MOTIVATION

The table here mentions statistics derived for the various groups of girls on the basis of the scores obtained on Achievement Motivation.

Table 8 : Statistics for Groups on Achievement Motivation

Groups		Girls-Working Mothers			Girls-Non Working Mothers		
		N	Mean	S.D.	N	Mean	S.D.
Pre-pubertal	9	50	50.50	5.41	50	48.96	6.13
Pre-pubertal	11	50	52.12	4.16	50	52.70	3.29
Pubertal	13	50	51.64	4.43	50	53.48	3.38

Table 9 : Analysis of Variance for Groups on Achievement Motivation

Source of variation	df	Sums of Squares	Mean Square (Variance)	F
Between Means	5	659.48	131.896	6.28**
Within Groups	294	6175.176	21.004	

** Significant at 0.01 level.

* Significant at 0.05 level.

The F-ratio derived here on the basis of Analysis of Variance is significant at 0.01 level, and shows that the performances of the groups of girls on the variable differ quite significantly. This encouraged further to calculate t values which have been reported below in the table.

Table 10 : Comparisons of Groups on Achievement Motivation

	Groups	Age	N	Mean	S.D.	t Value
A	Girls Working Mothers	9	50	50.50	5.41	AB = 1.68
B	Girls Working Mothers	11	50	52.12	4.16	AC=1.16
C	Girls Working Mothers	13	50	51.64	4.43	BC = 0.56
D	Girls Non-Working Mothers	9	50	48.96	6.13	DE=2.69**
E	Girls Non-Working Mothers	11	50	52.70	3.29	DF=4.61**
F	Girls Non-Working Mothers	13	50	53.48	3.38	EF=1.16
						AD=1.06
						BE=0.77
						CF=2.36*

**Significant at 0.01 level

* Significant at 0.05 level

Analysis and Interpretation

In this table only three t values are significant. Of these two are significant at 0.01 level and one at 0.05 level. This helps to report as follows:

1. Since the vertical comparisons of the means related with the gropus of girls at the various stages of development do not disclose anything, being close to each other, it can be said that practically at all the three age levels the Achievement Motivation among the groups of girls residing with working mothers is more or less the same.

2. On the other hand, the means obtained on this variable have gone rising in the positive direction. Side by side with age of course the mean obtained for the age group 13 is only slightly higher than that of age 11. This shows that by the time the girls of this group attain the age of 11, their Acvievement Motivation

is quite high. Moreover this level of Achievement Motivation is maintained by the girls of this group even up to the age of 13.

3. The agewise comparisons do not give anything worth mentioning for the age groups of 9 and 11. But for the age group of 13 the comparison of the means shows that Achievement Motivation among the girls residing with the non-working mothers is significantly much higher than that of the girls residing with the working mothers.

The rising trend in Achievement Motivation among girls residing with the non-working mothers helps to conclude that the presence of the mothers at home somehow provides these girls with an opportunity where they attempt to achieve more and more. On the other hand, probabely such opportunities are not available to the girls residing with the working mothers.

2. MANIFEST ANXIETY

The table below gives statistics derived on the basis of the scores obtained by the various groups of girls on "Anxiety".

Table 11. Statistics for Groups on Manifest Anxiety

Groups		Girls-Working Mothers			Girls-Non Working Mothers		
		N	Mean	S.D.	N	Mean	S.D.
Pre-pubertal	9	50	23.24	7.46	50	23.86	7.66
Pre-pubertal	11	50	26.10	7.34	50	25.08	7.28
Pubertal	13	50	29.14	7.90	50	26.92	7.43

Table 12. Analysis of Variance for Groups on Manifest Anxiety

Source of variation	df	Sums of Squares	Mean Square (Variance)	F
Between Means	5	681.02	136.204	2.41**
Within Groups	294	16601.988	56.47	

** Significant at 0.01 level.

* Significant at 0.05 level.

The F-ratio obtained here on the basis of Analysis of Variance is significant at 0.05 level. This shows that the performance of some groups of girls differs significantly from each other on this variable of the study. In order to find out which of the groups of girls differ significantly, t values were calculated and they have been reported in the following table.

Table 13 : Comparisons of Groups on Manifest Anxiety

	Groups	Age	N	Mean	S.D.	t Value
A	Girls Working Mothers	9	50	23.24	7.46	AB =1.93
B	Girls Working Mothers	11	50	26.10	7.34	AC=3.85**
C	Girls Working Mothers	13	50	29.14	7.90	BC=2.00*
D	Girls Non-Working Mothers	9	50	23.86	7.66	DE=0.82
E	Girls Non-Working Mothers	11	50	25.08	7.28	DF=2.03*
F	Girls Non-Working Mothers	13	50	26.92	7.43	EF=1.25
	**Significant at 0.01 level					AD=0.41
	* Significant at 0.05 level					BE=0.69
						CF=1.45

Analysis and Interpretation

In this table only three t values are significant, one at 0.01 level and two at 0.05 level. All these three are related with the vertical comparisons. None is significant for horizontal comparisons. This helps to interpret as folloes:

1. The vertical comparisons for the girls residing with the working mothers show that the means for age group of 9 and 11 do not differ significantly. On the other hand means related with the girls belonging to age group of 9 and 13, and of the age group of 11 and 13 differ significantly. This shows that the Anxiety level does not differ significantly among the girls who belong to age group of 9 and 11. But by the time the girls attain the age of 13 years, the Anxiety significantly increases among them as compared to the age of 9 and 11.
2. The vertical comparisons of the means belonging to the girls who reside with non-working mothers show that significant

differences appear only between the means related with the age group 9 and 13. Practically this also shows that Anxiety level does not increase significantly among the girls up to the age of 11, but it definitely increases by the time they attain the age of 13.

3. The agewise comparisons for the girls belonging to the working mothers and non-working mothers do not give any point worth mentioning. It can be generalized here that the presence of anxiety is highly noted among the girls at the age of 13 in both the groups of the girls probably due to the fact that they are attaining the age of puberty which in itself creats some tensions due to the physiological changes more among the girls.

3. SELF CONCEPT

The table below gives statistics derived on the basis of the scores obtained on Self Concept by the various groups of girls.

Table 14 : Statistics for Groups on Self Concept

Groups		Girls-Working Mothers			Girls-Non Working Mothers		
		N	Mean	S.D.	N	Mean	S.D.
Pre-pubertal	9	50	31.88	7.70	50	30.90	6.82
Pre-pubertal	11	50	32.90	9.07	50	32.72	6.77
Pubertal	13	50	32.56	6.55	50	37.08	6.11

Table 15 : Analysis of Variance for Groups on Self Concept

Source of variation	df	Sums of Squares	Mean Square (Variance)	F
Between Means	5	1129.63	225.926	
Within Groups	294	15392.6052	52.3558	4.32**

** Significant at 0.01 level.

* Significant at 0.05 level.

The F-ratio mentioned here derived on the basis of Anlysis of Variance is significant at 0.01 level. This shows that the performances of some groups of girls differ significantly and widely on this variable of the study. To find out where the groups differ, t values were calculated and these have been reported in the table below.

Table 16 : Comparisons of Groups on Self Concept

	Groups	Age	N	Mean	S.D.	t Value
A	Girls Working Mothers	9	50	31.88	7.70	AB =0.61
B	Girls Working Mothers	11	50	32.90	9.07	AC=0.48
C	Girls Working Mothers	13	50	32.56	6.55	BC=0.22
D	Girls Non-Working Mothers	9	50	30.90	6.82	DE=1.34
E	Girls Non-Working Mothers	11	50	32.72	6.77	DF=4.79**
F	Girls Non-Working Mothers	13	50	37.08	6.11	EF=3.38**
	**Significant at 0.01 level					AD=0.68
	* Significant at 0.05 level					BE=0.11
						CF=3.56**

Analysis and Interpretation

In the table mentioned above three t values are significant. All these are significant at 0.01 level, of these two are significant related with the comparisons of the groups of girls residing with the non-working mothers, and one is significant related with the agewise differences of the groups of girls residing with the working and non-working mothers. None is significant related with the groups of girls residing with working mothers. This helps to report as follows:

1. The study of the means obtained for the three groups of girls residing with working mothers shows that even at various age levels they are very close to each other. This shows that the development of self concept has not been influenced at the various stages of development in any way. The stature of self concept is the same at the three age levels.
2. On the other hand the means obtained for the girls residing with non-working mothers differ very significantly. The mean obtained for tha age group 13 is quite high comparatively as compared to the means obtained for the age group of 9 and 11. This refers to the fact that by the time the girls reach the age of 13, their self concept develops quite appreciably.

3. The two means obtained for the age groups of 9 and for the age groups of 11 years do not differ. Against this the means obtained for the age group of 13 differ quite significantly. In this case the mean obtained for the girls residing with the non-working mothers is significantly high. This helps to conclude that the self concept of the girls residibg with the non-working mothers is comparatively much enriched and developed as compared to the self concept of the girls residing with the working mothers.

The development of self concept is often much affected by the feeling of self regard and analysis of self by the person concerned and also by those with whom one comes in contact with. The above situation might have developd due to the reasons that the working mothers might not be getting much opportunities to help their daughters in having analysis of self. On the other hand such opportunities are very easily available to such non-working mothers who are conscious of the fact that their daughters must develop good "self" to become good housewives.

4. MATURITY

A. Intellecutual Maturity

The table below gives statistics obtained on the basis of the scores achieved by various groups of girls on 'Intellectual Maturity'.

Table 17 : Statistics for Groups on Intellectual Maturity

Groups		Girls-Working Mothers			Girls-Non Working Mothers		
		N	Mean	S.D.	N	Mean	S.D.
Pre-pubertal	9	50	39.86	6.31	50	38.30	5.39
Pre-pubertal	11	50	37.46	6.25	50	37.98	5.35
Pubertal	13	50	35.18	4.78	50	37.76	4.25

Table 18 : Analysis of Variance for Groups on Intellectual Maturity

Source of variation	df	Sums of Squares	Mean Square (Variance)	F
Between Means	5	570.77	114.154	
Within Groups	294	8695.7409	29.5773	3.86**

** Significant at 0.01 level.

* Significant at 0.05 level.

The F-ratio calculated here on the basis of Analysis of variance is significant at 0.01 level. This shows that on this variable some means are differing significantly.

To find out where such differences occur t values were calculated and they have been reported below in the table

Table 19 : Comparisons of Groups on Intellectual Maturity

	Groups	Age	N	Mean	S.D.	t Value
A	Girls Working Mothers	9	50	39.86	6.31	AB =1.92
B	Girls Working Mothers	11	50	37.46	6.25	AC=4.18**
C	Girls Working Mothers	13	50	35.18	4.78	BC=2.05*
D	Girls Non-Working Mothers	9	50	38.30	5.39	DE=0.36
E	Girls Non-Working Mothers	11	50	37.98	5.35	DF=0.56
F	Girls Non-Working Mothers	13	50	37.76	4.25	EF=0.23
	**Significant at 0.01 level * Significant at 0.05 level					AD=1.33 BE=0.45 CF=2.87**

Analysis and Interpretation

In this table three t values are significant. Of these one is significant at 0.05 level and two are significant at 0.01 level, here none is significant for the developmental comparisons of the girls residing with non-working mothers. This helps to interpret as follows:

1. The vertical comparisons of the means for groups of girls residing with working mothers reflect very interesting trend. Somehow with the stages of development the means for Intellectual Maturity for the groups of girls residing with the working mothers are going significantly down with age. This shows that Intellectual Maturity with rise in age has decreased. The girls at the age of 13 have displayed significantly quite a low Intellectual Maturity as compared to that of at age 9.
2. On the other hand the three means obtained for three age groups of girls residing with non-working mothers do not differ in any

way. This shows that these girls have displayed same level of Intellectual Maturity at all the three age levels.

3. The agewise comparisons disclose only one point. Among the two groups of girls, the girls of age group 13 residing with non-working mothers have displayed comparatively and significantly more Intellectual Maturity as compared to those who reside with working mothers at this age.

The conclusion drawn here on the basis of the performances on this variable seems to be an interesting one. If we at all believe that Intellectual Maturity once attained does not easily decrease, it may be interpreted here that the girls residing with the working mothers, due to more work at home in the absence of mothers, get very few opportunities to display their Intellectual Maturity. In addition to this in the absence of mothers, careless trends among girls also develop.

B. Emotional Maturity

The table below gives statistics derived on the basis of the scores achieved by the various groups of girls on 'Emotional Maturity'.

Table 20 : Statistics for Groups on Emotional Maturity

Groups		Girls-Working Mothers			Girls-Non Working Mothers		
		N	Mean	S.D.	N	Mean	S.D.
Pre-pubertal	9	50	38.92	7.07	50	37.22	6.53
Pre-pubertal	11	50	34.72	7.72	50	34.88	6.68
Pubertal	13	50	33.98	6.87	50	36.52	6.14

Table 21 : Analysis of Variance for Groups on Emotional Maturity

Source of variation	df	Sums of Squares	Mean Square (Variance)	F
Between Means	5	862.44	172.488	3.67**
Within Groups	294	13805.411	46.9572	

** Significant at 0.01 level.

* Significant at 0.05 level.

The F-ratio mentioned above in the table is significant at 0.01 level. This shows that some groups differ significantly in their performance on this variable of study. So, in order to locate which of the groups differ in this regard, t values were calculated and these have been reported below in the table.

Table 22 Comparisons of Groups on Emotional Maturity

	Groups	Age	N	Mean	S.D.	t Value
A	Girls Working Mothers	9	50	38.92	7.07	AB =2.83**
B	Girls Working Mothers	11	50	34.72	7.72	AC=3.55**
C	Girls Working Mothers	13	50	33.98	6.87	BC=0.50
D	Girls Non-Working Mothers	9	50	37.22	6.53	DE=1.77
E	Girls Non-Working Mothers	11	50	34.88	6.68	DF=0.55
F	Girls Non-Working Mothers	13	50	36.52	6.14	EF=1.28
	**Significant at 0.01 level * Significant at 0.05 level					AD=1.25
						BE=0.11
						CF=1.95

Analysis and Interpretation

In this table only two t values are significant. These are significant at 0.01 level and are related with the girls residing with the working mothers. This helps to conclude as follows:

1. The vertical comparisons for the groups of girls residing with the working mothers show that the means obtained for the groups of girls of age 11 and age 13 are significantly low than that obtained for the group of girls aged 9. This shows that the Emotional Maturity has decreased among these two groups of girls with the rise in age and with the onset of puberty.
2. The comparison of the three means obtained for the girls residing with non-working mothers refering to the three stages of development does not reflect any downward or upward trend. This shows that at all the three different age levels the groups of girls residing with the non-working mothers have displayed practically the same level of Emotional Maturity.

3. The agewise comparisons between the girls residing with working and non-working mothers also do not disclose anything worth mentioning. In other words this reflects that at the three age leves, comparatively both the groups of girls display more or less same level of Emotional Maturity.

The downward trend with rise of age in Emotional Maturity for the girls residing with working mothers might be due to the fact that their daughters might not be getting any guidance for the control of negative emotions, especially the fear which often is reflected in the behaviour of girls with the onset of puberty due to physiological disturbances. Such guidance is more available to the girls who reside with non-working mothers.

C. Social Maturity

The table below gives statistics obtained on the basis of the scores achieved by the various groups of girls on 'Social Maturity'.

Table 23: Statistics for Groups on Social Maturity

Groups		Girls-Working Mothers			Girls-Non Working Mothers		
		N	Mean	S.D.	N	Mean	S.D.
Pre-pubertal	9	50	39.74	7.81	50	37.40	6.31
Pre-pubertal	11	50	37.18	6.02	50	37.44	5.68
Pubertal	13	50	37.28	5.76	50	36.54	5.51

Table 24 : Analysis of Variance for Groups on Social Maturity

Source of variation	df	Sums of Squares	Mean Square (Variance)	F
Between Means	5	325.39	65.078	1.67
Within Groups	294	11017.782	38.795	

** Significant at 0.01 level. * Significant at 0.05 level.

The F-ratio mentioned here in the table is not significant. This shows that for both the groups of girls the means obtained for the various stages of development do not differ significantly. Also, the means for the various age groups reflecting horizontal comparisons do not differ. This helps to conclude that among all the groups of girls Social Maturity is more or less present at the same level.

Comparisons of Girls Residing with Working and Non-Working Mothers

(Motivational Variables)

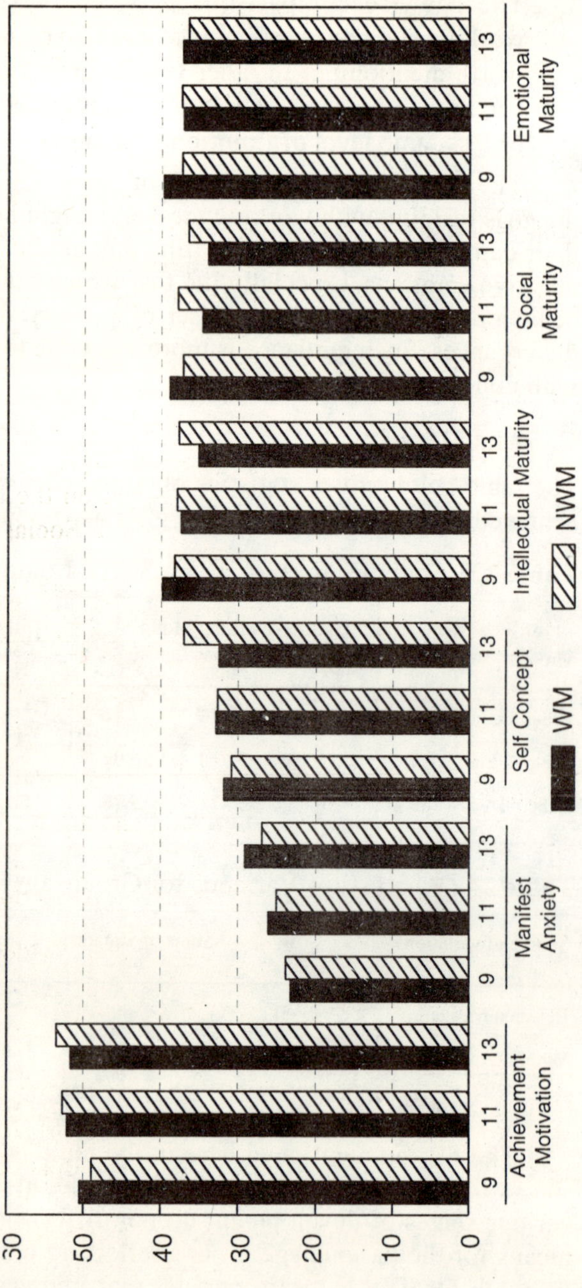

PART B

STUDY OF PERSONALITY VARIABLES

It may be recalled here that under personality variables, only two variables have been selected here for the study. These are Personality Factors as described by 'Cattell',and Reactions to Frustrations as described by Saul Rosenzweig.As mentioned in chapter II, personality factors have been studied with the help of Cattell's children's personality Questionnaire (CPQ) and Reactions to Frustrations have been studied with the help of Picture Frustration Study (PF) by Udai Preek and Saul Rosenzweig. The description of these tests is already available in chapter II.

The study has been presented here in this very order. It may be mentioned here that PF study is a Projective Test of studying one's personality.

FACTOR A - Reserved vs Warmhearted

The table below gives statistics derived on the basis of the scores obtained by the different groups of girls on factor A.

Table 25: Statistics for Groups on Factor A

Groups		Girls-Working Mothers			Girls-Non Working Mothers		
		N	Mean	S.D.	N	Mean	S.D.
Pre-pubertal	9	50	6.74	1.28	50	6.26	1.72
Pre-pubertal	11	50	6.62	1.62	50	6.48	1.46
Pubertal	13	50	6.20	1.52	50	6.38	1.71

Table 26: Analysis of Variance for Groups on Factor A

Source of variation	df	Sums of Squares	Mean Square (Variance)	F
Between Means	5	10.87	2.174	
Within Groups	294	714.7774	2.4312	0.894

** Significant at 0.01 level.

* Significant at 0.05 level.

The F-ratio obtained here on the Analysis of Variance is insignificant. This shows that the means mentioned above in the table do not differ significantly from each other, refering to the fact that this personality trait is more or less equally present among all the groups of girls. In other words it can be interpreted that the girls residing with the working mothers and the girls residing with the non-working mothers are equally warmhearted at all the stages of development.

FACTOR B - Dull vs Bright

The table below gives statistics derived on the basis of the scores obtained by different groups of girls on factor B.

Table 27 : Statistics for Groups on Factor B

Groups		Girls-Working Mothers			Girls-Non Working Mothers		
		N	Mean	S.D.	N	Mean	S.D.
Pre-pubertal	9	50	4.28	1.46	50	4.10	1.69
Pre-pubertal	11	50	4.43	1.62	50	4.32	1.70
Pubertal	13	50	4.52	1.56	50	4.49	1.84

Table 28: Analysis of Variance for Groups on Factor B

Source of variation	df	Sums of Squares	Mean Square (Variance)	F
Between Means	5	6.16	1.232	
Within Groups	294	799.74	2.72	0.452

** Significant at 0.01 level.

* Significant at 0.05 level.

The F-ratio obtained here on the basis of Analysis of Variance is insignificant. This shows that different means do not differ significantly from each other on factor B.So it can be interpreted that the different groups of girls do not differ from each other on this factor.

This may be due to the fact that factor B of CPQ refers to 'Intelligence' and at the start all these groups were already equated on the basis of intelligence with a view to control this variable.

FACTOR C - Affected by Feelings vs Emotionally Stable

The table below provides statistics based on the scores obtained by the various groups of girls on factor C.

Table 29 Statistics for Groups on Factor C

Groups		Girls-Working Mothers			Girls-Non Working Mothers		
		N	Mean	S.D.	N	Mean	S.D.
Pre-pubertal	9	50	7.00	1.79	50	6.96	1.49
Pre-pubertal	11	50	6.74	1.84	50	6.62	1.76
Pubertal	13	50	6.24	1.71	50	6.64	1.81

Table 30: Analysis of Variance for Groups on Factor C

Source of variation	df	Sums of Squares	Mean Square (Variance)	F
Between Means	5	11.99	2.398	
Within Groups	294	887.2724	3.02	0.79

** Significant at 0.01 level.

* Significant at 0.05 level.

The F-ratio obtained here on the basis of Anlysis of Variance is insignificant. This shows that the means mentioned above do not differ significantly from each other on this factor, refering to the fact that all the groups of girls seem to be Emotionally stable more or less equally.

FACTOR D - Phlegmatic vs Excitable

The table below gives statistics derived on the basis of scores obtained by various groups of girls on factor D.

Table 31 Statistics for Groups on Factor D

Groups		Girls-Working Mothers			Girls-Non Working Mothers		
		N	Mean	S.D.	N	Mean	S.D.
Pre-pubertal	9	50	3.18	1.54	50	2.88	1.46
Pre-pubertal	11	50	3.14	1.66	50	2.72	1.13
Pubertal	13	50	3.62	1.96	50	3.32	1.78

Table 32: Analysis of Variance for Groups on Factor D

Source of variation	df	Sums of Squares	Mean Square (Variance)	F
Between Means	5	25.42	5.084	
Within Groups	294	761.7394	2.5910	1.96

** Significant at 0.01 level.

* Significant at 0.05 level.

The F-ratio obtained here on the basis of Analysis of variance is insignificant. This shows that the means related with this factor mentioned above do not differ significantly from each other.

This helps to conclude that as for as this trait is concerned, practically all the groups are at the same level, and equally phlegmatic.

FACTOR E - Obedient vs Dominant

The table below gives statistics derived on the basis of scores obtained by the groups of girls on factor E.

Table 33 Statistics for Groups on Factor E

Groups		Girls-Working Mothers			Girls-Non Working Mothers		
		N	Mean	S.D.	N	Mean	S.D.
Pre-pubertal	9	50	3.58	1.64	50	2.90	1.36
Pre-pubertal	11	50	3.08	1.53	50	2.98	1.53
Pubertal	13	50	3.76	1.32	50	3.26	1.47

Table 34 Analysis of Variance for Groups on Factor E

Source of variation	df	Sums of Squares	Mean Square (Variance)	F
Between Means	5	29.64	5.928	
Within Groups	294	643.0907	2.187	2.71*

** Significant at 0.01 level.

* Significant at 0.05 level.

The F-ratio calculated here on the basis of Analysis of Variance is significant at 0.05 level. This shows that some of the means mentioned above differ significantly, refering to the fact that some of the groups differ significantly in their performance on this factor.

To find out which of the groups differ, t values were calculated and these have been reported below.

Table 35: Comparisons of Groups on Factor E

	Groups	Age	N	Mean	S.D.	t Value
A	Girls Working Mothers	9	50	3.58	1.64	AB =1.61
B	Girls Working Mothers	11	50	3.08	1.53	AC=0.60
C	Girls Working Mothers	13	50	3.76	1.32	BC=2.43*
D	Girls Non-Working Mothers	9	50	2.90	1.36	DE=0.27
E	Girls Non-Working Mothers	11	50	2.98	1.53	DF=1.28
F	Girls Non-Working Mothers	13	50	3.26	1.47	EF=0.93
						AD=2.27*
						BE=0.33
						CF=1.85

**Significant at 0.01 level
* Significant at 0.05 level

Analysis and Interpretation

In this table only two t values are significant. These are significant at 0.05 level. This helps to conclude as follows:

1. The vertical comparisons of the means show that at the various stages of development and age levels the means refering to the performance of the girls residing with the working mothers have not moved much in either direction on this factor, except at age 13 as compaired to 11. This shows that on this personality variable some development is noted but it is very nominal though significant.
2. The vertical comparisons of the means refering to the performance of the girls residing with the non-working mothers show that on this factor all the three groups of girls are equally mild and accomodating.

3. The agewise comparisons do not give anything worth mentioning for age 11 and age 13. It is only for age 9 where the two means for the two groups of girls residing with working mothers and non-working mothers differ significantly. Here the mean obtained for girls residing with non-working mothers is significantly low, refering to low score description. This shows that comparatively the girls residing with non-working mothers are more obedient, mild and accomodating.

Practically this trait is more or less equally present among all the groups of girls. If there are some differences they are very minor. Still, one can notice that girls residing with non- working mothers at the earlier stages of development are comparatively more mild and accomodating. But at the further stages of development all the groups possess the trait at equal level. This shows that with entry into the adolescence period, the consciousness among all the girls makes them equally mild and accomodating.

FACTOR F - Sober vs Enthusiastic

The table below gives statistics derived on the basis of scores obtained by the various groups of girls on factor F.

Table 36: Statistics for Groups on Factor F

Groups		Girls-Working Mothers			Girls-Non Working Mothers		
		N	Mean	S.D.	N	Mean	S.D.
Pre-pubertal	9	50	4.32	1.46	50	3.42	1.39
Pre-pubertal	11	50	5.70	2.25	50	4.36	1.56
Pubertal	13	50	5.28	1.83	50	4.72	1.46

Table 37: Analysis of Variance for Groups on Factor F

Source of variation	df	Sums of Squares	Mean Square (Variance)	F
Between Means	5	160.43	32.086	
Within Groups	294	839.6052	2.8558	11.24**

** Significant at 0.01 level.

* Significant at 0.05 level.

The F-ratio obtained here on the basis of Analysis of Variance is significant at 0.01 level. This shows that on this factor, the means refering to the performance of the girls differ significantly. As a result of this t values have been calculated and they have been reported in the table below.

Table 33: Comparisons of Groups on Factor F

	Groups	Age	N	Mean	S.D.	t Value
A	Girls Working Mothers	9	50	4.32	1.46	AB =3.63*
B	Girls Working Mothers	11	50	5.70	2.25	AC=2.90**
C	Girls Working Mothers	13	50	5.28	1.83	BC=1.02
D	Girls Non-Working Mothers	9	50	3.42	1.39	DE=3.13**
E	Girls Non-Working Mothers	11	50	4.36	1.59	DF=4.48**
F	Girls Non-Working Mothers	13	50	4.72	1.46	EF=1.16
	**Significant at 0.01 level					AD=3.10**
	* Significant at 0.05 level					BE=3.43**
						CF=1.69

Analysis and Interpretation

This table reports six t values as significant. All these are significant at 0.01 level. This helps to conclude as follows:

1. The vertical comparisons of the means obtained by the girls residing with the working mothers show that significant differences occur with rising age. The scores are significantly going upward. This shows that there is a trend among the girls of this group from soberity to enthusiasm.

2. The vertical comparisons of the means obtained for the girls residing with the non-working mothers also diclose the same phenomenon. Here too with rise in age from 9 to 13 the girls are moving towards enthusiasm from soberity.

3. The agewise comparisons show that the means for the two groups are differing significantly for the age group of 9 and again for the age group of 11 and not for the age group of 13. Since the means for the earlier ages are significantly higher for girls residing with working mothers, it can be said that trend

from soberity to enthusiasm is comparatively more among the girls residing with the working mothers.

This shows that practically all the girls have displayed a trend on this factor, which shows that with rise in age the girls are marching from soberity to enthusiasm but at the earlier stages it is more among the girls residing with the working mothers. This may be due to the fact, because the girls residing with the working mothers get more independent hours to take risks and face enthusiasm.

FACTOR G - Expedient vs Conscientious

The table below gives statistics based on scores obtained by the various groups of girls on factor G.

Table 39: Statistics for Groups on Factor G

Groups		Girls-Working Mothers			Girls-Non Working Mothers		
		N	Mean	S.D.	N	Mean	S.D.
Pre-pubertal	9	50	7.46	1.84	50	7.42	1.72
Pre-pubertal	11	50	7.36	1.64	50	7.74	1.35
Pubertal	13	50	6.82	1.61	50	7.00	2.01

Table 40: Analysis of Variance for Groups on Factor G

Source of variation	df	Sums of Squares	Mean Square (Variance)	F
Between Means	5	25.11	5.022	
Within Groups	294	856.9267	2.9147	1.72

** Significant at 0.01 level.

* Significant at 0.05 level.

The F-ratio obtained here on the basis of Analysis of Variance is not significant. This shows that the means above in the table do not differ significantly.

Since the scores have a trend towards high score description, this shows that practically among all the girls there is consciousness to regard rules.

FACTOR H - Shy vs Venturesome

The table below gives statistics derived on the basis of the scores obtained by various groups of girls on factor H.

Table 41: Statistics for Groups on Factor H

Groups		Girls-Working Mothers			Girls-Non Working Mothers		
		N	Mean	S.D.	N	Mean	S.D.
Pre-pubertal	9	50	6.80	1.37	50	6.16	1.65
Pre-pubertal	11	50	5.62	1.51	50	6.00	1.54
Pubertal	13	50	5.82	1.46	50	5.94	1.62

Table 42: Analysis of Variance for Groups on Factor H

Source of variation	df	Sums of Squares	Mean Square (Variance)	F
Between Means	5	41.35	8.27	
Within Groups	294	686.3479	2.3345	3.54**

** Significant at 0.01 level.

* Significant at 0.05 level.

The F-ratio obtained here on the basis of Analysis of Variance is significant at 0.01 level. This shows that some of the means differ significantly.To find out which of the groups differ, the t values were calculated and these have been presented in the table below.

Table 43: Comparisons of Groups on Factor H

	Groups	Age	N	Mean	S.D.	t Value
A	Girls Working Mothers	9	50	6.80	1.37	AB =4.07**
B	Girls Working Mothers	11	50	5.62	1.51	AC=3.50**
C	Girls Working Mothers	13	50	5.82	1.46	BC=0.67
D	Girls Non-Working Mothers	9	50	6.16	1.65	DE=0.50
E	Girls Non-Working Mothers	11	50	6.00	1.54	DF=0.69
F	Girls Non-Working Mothers	13	50	5.94	1.62	EF=0.19
	**Significant at 0.01 level					AD=2.13*
	* Significant at 0.05 level					BE=1.22
						CF=0.39

Analysis and Interpretation

In this table three t values are significant. This helps to interpret as follows:

1. The developmental comparisons of the means for the girls residing with the working mothers show that the scores are decreasing with rising age. This shows that the girls are developing a tendency to move towards shyness with rise in age.
2. In the case of the girls residing with the non-working mothers the three means for the three age groups do not differ significantly. They are also very close to each other. This shows that this trait is equally present among all the groups.
3. The agewise comparisons show that at age 9 the girls residing with the working mothers are significantly more socially bold and uninhibited than those who reside with the non-working mothers. At further age groups this thing is not noted.

This helps to conclude that at the earlier stages of development girls residing with the working mothers feel more socially bold and uninhibited probabely because they have less restrictions and more of freedom to work independently in the absence of mothers who are out practically to go on job.comparatively these girls have to take more of decisions themselves.

FACTOR I - Tough Mindedness vs Tender Mindedness

The table below gives statistics derived on the basis of scores obtained by various groups of girls on factor I.

Table 44: Statistics for Groups on Factor I

Groups		Girls-Working Mothers			Girls-Non Working Mothers		
		N	Mean	S.D.	N	Mean	S.D.
Pre-pubertal	9	50	5.34	1.44	50	5.88	1.63
Pre-pubertal	11	50	5.24	1.35	50	5.06	1.30
Pubertal	13	50	4.60	1.37	50	4.94	1.43

Table 45: Analysis of Variance for Groups on Factor I

Source of variation	df	Sums of Squares	Mean Square (Variance)	F
Between Means	5	46.39	9.278	
Within Groups	294	608.24	2.058	4.51**

** Significant at 0.01 level.
* Significant at 0.05 level.

The F-ratio obtained here on the basis ofAnalysis of Variance is significant at 0.01 level. This shows that some of the groups differ significantly in their performance on this variable of study.

Further t values were calculated to find out the groups which differ significantly from each other. These values are given in the table below.

Table 46: Comparisons of Groups on Factor I

	Groups	Age	N	Mean	S.D.	t Value
A	Girls Working Mothers	9	50	5.34	1.44	AB =0.36
B	Girls Working Mothers	11	50	5.24	1.35	AC=2.64**
C	Girls Working Mothers	13	50	4.60	1.37	BC=2.37*
D	Girls Non-Working Mothers	9	50	5.88	1.63	DE=2.83**
E	Girls Non-Working Mothers	11	50	5.06	1.30	DF=3.03**
F	Girls Non-Working Mothers	13	50	4.94	1.43	EF=0.44
	**Significant at 0.01 level					AD=1.74
	* Significant at 0.05 level					BE=0.67
						CF=1.21

Analysis and Interpretation

In the above mentioned table four t values are significant, one at 0.05 level and three at 0.01 level. This helps to interpret as follows:

1. The developmental comparisons of the means show that among the girls residing with the working mothers there is a trend to move towards tough mindedness from tender mindedness with the rise in age.

2. In the case of girls residing with the non-working mothers the above trend and phenomenon is also present. Here too the scores are significantly decreasing with rising age. This shows that with onset of puberty and entry into adolescence they are getting more tough minded.
3. The agewise comparisons do not report anything significant and worth reporting. Both the groups of girls at three age group levels have displayed this trait more or less at equal level. In both the cases it has been noted that inspite of the circumstances with rise in age the girls are getting more tough minded. This may be because that they have to face more of realities with rise in age and at times they have to learn to be tough minded to face the realities of life.

FACTOR J - Zestful vs Circumspect Individualism

The following table gives statistics derived on the basis of scores obtained by the various groups of girls on factor J. Analysis of Variance follows.

Table 47: Statistics for Groups on Factor J

Groups		Girls-Working Mothers			Girls-Non Working Mothers		
		N	Mean	S.D.	N	Mean	S.D.
Pre-pubertal	9	50	4.16	1.63	50	4.38	1.74
Pre-pubertal	11	50	4.68	1.70	50	4.62	1.75
Pubertal	13	50	5.12	1.48	50	5.20	1.57

Table 48: Analysis of Variance for Groups on Factor J

Source of variation	df	Sums of Squares	Mean Square (Variance)	F
Between Means	5	41.35	8.27	
Within Groups	294	798.3227	2.71	3.05*

** Significant at 0.01 level.

* Significant at 0.05 level.

The F-ratio obtained here is significant at 0.05 level. This shows that the various groups of girls differ significantly on this factor. So, t values were calculated to locate where the groups actually differ and these t values have been presented in the table below.

Table 49: Comparisons of Groups on Factor J

	Groups	Age	N	Mean	S.D.	t Value
A	Girls Working Mothers	9	50	4.16	1.63	AB =1.58
B	Girls Working Mothers	11	50	4.68	1.70	AC=3.10**
C	Girls Working Mothers	13	50	5.12	1.48	BC=1.38
D	Girls Non-Working Mothers	9	50	4.38	1.74	DE=0.68
E	Girls Non-Working Mothers	11	50	4.62	1.75	DF=2.48*
F	Girls Non-Working Mothers	13	50	5.20	1.57	EF=1.76
						AD=0.65
						BE=0.17
						CF=0.26

**Significant at 0.01 level
* Significant at 0.05 level

Analysis and Interpretation

Of the 9 t values, only two are significant. One is significant at 0.05 level and other one is significant at 0.01 level. This helps to conclude as follows:

1. The vertical comparisons show that the means for the age groups of 9 and 11 do not differ significantly but the means for the age groups of 9 and 13 differ significantly. The mean obtained for the girls of age group of 13 is significantly quite high. This helps to say that the girls of the working mothers in the process of their development like group action and remain vigorous or zestful up to the age of 11 but by the time they reach or attain the age of 13 they start becoming internally restrained.
2. This thing is also reflected in the process of development of the girls who reside with the non-working mothers. They also remain equally zestful at the age of 9 and at the age of 11 but with the onset of puberty on reaching the age of 13 they also become internally restrained.

3. The agewise comparisons do not disclose any significant differences at any age. This shows that among both the groups of girls the trend on this factor are more or less the same at all the ages.

This helps to interpret that on this factor the display of the girls residing with the working mothers and of those who reside with the non-working mothers is more or less the same in the process of development, and is not affected by the environmental situations.

FACTOR N - Forthright vs Shrewd

The following table gives the statistics based on scores obtained by various groups of girls on factor N of CPQ. The analysis of variance follows further.

Table 50 Statistics for Groups on Factor N

Groups		Girls-Working Mothers			Girls-Non Working Mothers		
		N	Mean	S.D.	N	Mean	S.D.
Pre-pubertal	9	50	3.04	1.28	50	3.02	1.87
Pre-pubertal	11	50	3.14	1.75	50	2.74	1.35
Pubertal	13	50	3.72	1.66	50	3.02	1.60

Table 51 Analysis of Variance for Groups on Factor N

Source of variation	df	Sums of Squares	Mean Square (Variance)	F
Between Means	5	26.55	5.31	
Within Groups	294	751.4591	2.55	2.08

** Significant at 0.01 level.

* Significant at 0.05 level.

The F-ratio obtained here is not significant at any level. This shows that the means obtained for girls of different groups do not differ significantly of factor N, meaning thereby that their performance on the factor N is more or less the same.

This helps to interpret that since practically all the means refer to low score description, all the groups of girls under both the environmental situations are forthright or natural in their behaviour.

FACTOR O - Self Assured vs Guilt Prone

The table below gives statistics derived on the basis of scores obtained by the various groups of girls on factor O of CPQ.

Table 52: Statistics for Groups on Factor O

Groups		Girls-Working Mothers			Girls-Non Working Mothers		
		N	Mean	S.D.	N	Mean	S.D.
Pre-pubertal	9	50	2.98	1.75	50	3.08	1.61
Pre-pubertal	11	50	3.54	1.77	50	3.10	1.50
Pubertal	13	50	4.40	1.81	50	4.02	2.00

Table 53: Analysis of Variance for Groups on Factor O

Source of variation	df	Sums of Squares	Mean Square (Variance)	F
Between Means	5	84.32	16.864	
Within Groups	294	897.3664	3.053	5.52**

** Significant at 0.01 level.

* Significant at 0.05 level.

The F-ratio obtained here is significant at 0.01 level. This shows that the performance of some groups of girls differ significantly from each other on this factor. In order to findout which of the groups of girls differ significantly, t values were calculated and they have been presented in the following table.

Table 54: Comparisons of Groups on Factor O

	Groups	Age	N	Mean	S.D.	t Value
A	Girls Working Mothers	9	50	2.98	1.75	AB =1.60
B	Girls Working Mothers	11	50	3.54	1.77	AC=3.94**
C	Girls Working Mothers	13	50	4.40	1.81	BC=2.32*
D	Girls Non-Working Mothers	9	50	3.08	1.61	DE=0.06
E	Girls Non-Working Mothers	11	50	3.10	1.50	DF=2.61*
F	Girls Non-Working Mothers	13	50	4.02	2.00	EF=2.63*
						AD=0.29
						BE=1.33
						CF=1.00

**Significant at 0.01 level
* Significant at 0.05 level

Analysis and Interpretation

In the above mentioned table only four t values are significant. Two are significant at 0.05 level and two are significant at 0.01 level. All these are related with the vertical comparisons. None is significant for horizontol comparisons. This helps to interpret as follows:

1. The vertical comparisons of the means obtained by the groups of girls residing with the working mothers disclose that on this factor the girls of age groups 9 and 11 do not differ in their display. But significant differences appear by the time the girls attain the age of 13. In other words it can be interpreted that in the begining the girls are self assured and less apprehensive, but with the rise in age they start becoming apprehensive.
2. The above position is also noted in the case of the girls who reside with the non-working mothers. The position of the means, being more or less the same, also helps to say that in the begining at the early stages of development the girls are less apprehensive but with the rise in age they slowly and slowly start becoming more apprehensive in nature.
3. The horizontal coparisons do not disclose anything at any age. On the other hand in can be said that at all ages here under the study the girls display on this factor is more or less the same.

At the end it can be said that the girls of both the groups are equally self assured at the early stages of development. Of course under both the situations they start moving towards apprehensiveness slowly and slowly. By the time they enter the pubertal age they become more apprehensive.

FACTOR Q3 - Undisciplined Self vs Controlled

The following table presents the statistics for different groups of girls on factor Q3. The analysis of variance follows:

Table 55: Statistics for Groups on Factor Q_3

Groups		Girls-Working Mothers			Girls-Non Working Mothers		
		N	Mean	S.D.	N	Mean	S.D.
Pre-pubertal	9	50	7.84	1.99	50	8.00	1.94
Pre-pubertal	11	50	7.58	1.81	50	7.90	2.02
Pubertal	13	50	5.54	1.64	50	7.78	1.77

Table 56: Analysis of Variance for Groups on Factor Q_3

Source of variation	df	Sums of Squares	Mean Square (Variance)	F
Between Means	5	168.27	33.654	
Within Groups	294	1024.2323	3.483	9.66**

** Significant at 0.01 level.

* Significant at 0.05 level.

The F-ratio obtained here is significant at 0.01 level. This shows that different groups of girls differ significantly on this trait.

This encouraged further to calculate t values which have been reported below in the table.

Table 57: Comparisons of Groups on Factor Q_3

	Groups	Age	N	Mean	S.D.	t Value
A	Girls Working Mothers	9	50	7.84	1.99	AB =0.68
B	Girls Working Mothers	11	50	7.58	1.81	AC=5.56**
C	Girls Working Mothers	13	50	5.84	1.64	BC=4.97**
D	Girls Non-Working Mothers	9	50	8.00	1.94	DE=0.26
E	Girls Non-Working Mothers	11	50	7.90	2.02	DF=0.59
F	Girls Non-Working Mothers	13	50	7.78	1.77	EF=0.31
						AD=0.41
						BE=0.84
						CF=5.70**

**Significant at 0.01 level
* Significant at 0.05 level

Analysis and Interpretation

In this table only three t values are significant. Theseare significant at 0.01 level. This helps to conclude as follows.

1. The vertical comparisons of the means refering to the performances of the girls residing with the working mothers disclose on this factor that at the age levels of 9 and 11 the girls are more or less equally controlled but with the onset of puberty and entry into the age of adolescence they start becoming uncontrolled and undisciplined and also follow own urges.
2. The means obtained by the girls residing with the non-working mothers do not differ significantly from each other. This shows that at all the three stages of development they are more or less equally controlled.
3. The agewise differences for both the groups are not significant for the age group of 9 and for the age group of 11. But among the groups of 13 years of age, significant difference are noted on this factor. The girls residing with the working mothers comparatively are less controlled, whereas the girls residing with the non-working mothers are more controlled and socially precise.

The study on this factor shows that by the time the girls enter the age of 13, those who reside with the non-working are controlled and socially precise in their behaviour. Whereas those who reside with the working mothers follow own urges and start displaying undisciplined behaviours. It may be due to the fact that due to being on jobs away from home, the working mothers do not get opportunity to look into the behaviours of their daughters. The result is that these girls feel more free to follow their own urges and do things as they like.

FACTOR Q4 - Relaxed vs Tense

The table below gives statistics derived on the basis of scores obtained on factor Q4 by thevarious groups of girls.

Table 58. Statistics for Groups on Factor Q4

Groups		Girls-Working Mothers			Girls-Non Working Mothers		
		N	Mean	S.D.	N	Mean	S.D.
Pre-pubertal	9	50	3.04	2.14	50	2.68	1.85
Pre-pubertal	11	50	3.08	1.86	50	2.98	2.09
Pubertal	13	50	4.20	2.04	50	3.06	1.88

Table 59: Analysis of Variance for Groups on Factor Q4

Source of variation	df	Sums of Squares	Mean Square (Variance)	F
Between Means	5	68.71	13.742	
Within Groups	294	1152.7642	3.92	3.51**

** Significant at 0.01 level.

* Significant at 0.05 level.

The F-ratio mentioned above on the basis of Analysis of variance is significant at 0.01 level. This shows that the performances of some groups of girls differ significantly on this trait. To find out where the groups differ, t values were calculated and these have been reported in the table below.

Table 60: Comparisons of Groups on Factor Q4

	Groups	Age	N	Mean	S.D.	t Value
A	Girls Working Mothers	9	50	3.04	2.14	AB =0.10
B	Girls Working Mothers	11	50	3.08	1.86	AC=2.76**
C	Girls Working Mothers	13	50	4.20	2.04	BC=2.87**
D	Girls Non-Working Mothers	9	50	2.68	1.85	DE=0.77
E	Girls Non-Working Mothers	11	50	2.98	2.09	DF=1.02
F	Girls Non-Working Mothers	13	50	3.06	1.88	EF=0.20
	**Significant at 0.01 level					AD=0.90
	* Significant at 0.05 level					BE=0.26
						CF=2.92**

Analysis and Interpretation

In this table only three t values are significant. All the three are significant at 0.01 level. This helps to report as follows:

1. The vertical comparisons of the means by the girls residing with the working mothers show that by the time they enter the age of 13 they slowly and slowly start becoming less relaxed and on the other hand start becoming tense.
2. This trend can also be seen slightly among the girls residing with the non-working mothers. But, since the three means for the three age groups do not differ significantly it can be said that at all the three age levels they are more or less equally relaxed.
3. The agewise differences for age group of 9 and for age group of 11 are not significant on this factor but at the age of 13, the position of the means disclose that the girls residing with the non-working mothers are much more relaxed than those who reside with the working mothers.

The study shows that girls under both the environmental situations display the same type of behaviour on this factor. But with the onset of puberty the situation changes.

The girls residing with the working mothers are comparatively less relaxed, probabely because at a number of occassions they might not be getting necessary guidance which on the other hand is available to the girls who reside with the non- working mothers.

Comparisons of Girls Residing with Working and Non-Working Mothers

(Personality Factors)

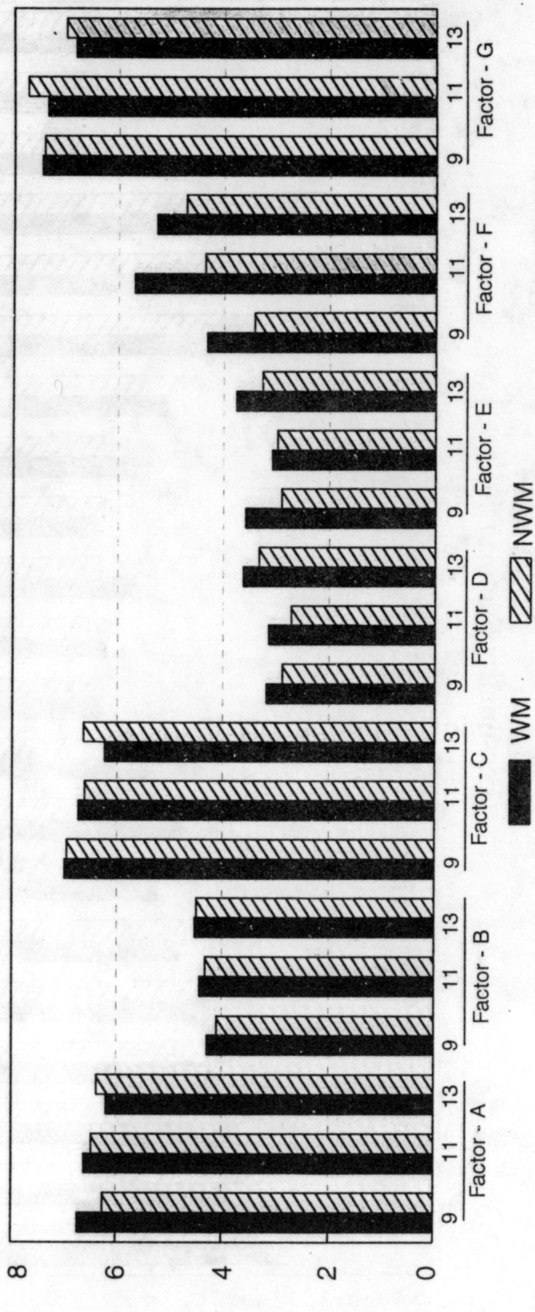

Comparisons of Girls Residing with Working and Non-Working Mothers

(Personality Factors)

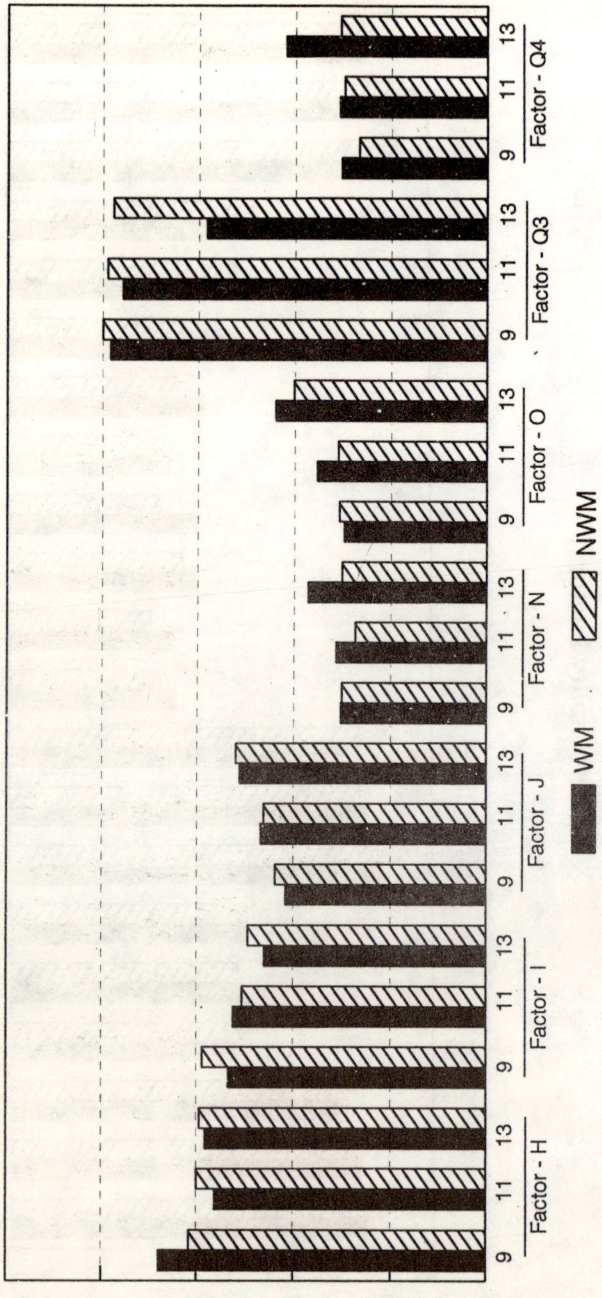

REACTIONS TO FRUSTRATION

A. OBSTACLE DOMINANCE

The table below given statistics derived on the basis of the scores obtained by the girls on Obstacle Dominance.

Table 61: Statistics for Groups on Obstacle Dominance

Groups		Girls-Working Mothers			Girls-Non Working Mothers		
		N	Mean	S.D.	N	Mean	S.D.
Pre-puberta:	9	50	3.90	1.15	50	3.98	1.36
Pre-pubertal	11	50	3.84	1.20	50	3.92	1.30
Pubertal	13	50	4.96	1.59	50	3.70	134

Table 62: Analysis of Variance for Groups on Obstacle Dominance

Source of variation	df	Sums of Squares	Mean Square (Variance)	F
Between Means	5	51.95	10.39	
Within Groups	294	520.66	1.77	5.87**

** Significant at 0.01 level.

* Significant at 0.05 level.

The F-ratio mentioned in the table is significant at 0.01 level. This shows that some groups of girls differ significantly on this variable in their performance.

In order to find out which of the groups differ in this regard t values were calculated and they have been presented below in the table.

Talbe 63: Comparisons of Groups on Obstacle Dominance

	Groups	Age	N	Mean	S.D.	t Value
A	Girls Working Mothers	9	50	3.90	1.15	AB =0.25
B	Girls Working Mothers	11	50	3.84	1.20	AC=3.78**
C	Girls Working Mothers	13	50	4.96	1.59	BC=4.00**
D	Girls Non-Working Mothers	9	50	3.98	1.36	DE=0.22
E	Girls Non-Working Mothers	11	50	3.92	1.30	DF=1.04
F	Girls Non-Working Mothers	13	50	3.70	1.34	EF=0.84
						AD=0.32
						BE=0.32
						CF=4.34**

**Significant at 0.01 level
* Significant at 0.05 level

Analysis and Interpretation

In this table three t values are significient. All these three are significient at 0.01. However they help to conclude as follows.

1. In the case of developmental comparisons for the groups of girls residing with working mothers it is noted that the mean obtained for the group of girls aged 13 is significantly high than that obtained for the groups of girls aged 9 years and aged 11 years. This shows that Obstacle Dominance is more or less equally present among the girls at age 9 and 11 but by the time the girls attain the age of 13, the Obstacle Dominance significantly increases in them.
2. The three means representing vertical comparisons at age 9 11 and 13 for the groups of girls residing with the non working mothers do not differ significantly from each other. This shows that at all these age levels among the groups of girls residing with the non-working mothers the presence of Obstacle Dominance is more or less the same.
3. The age wise comparisons of the means show that among both the groups of girls the display of Obstacle Dominance is more or less the same at age 9 and 11 but at age 13 it is clearly visible that Obstacle Dominance is more present and noticed among

the girls residing with the working mothers than those who reside with the non-working mothers.

The tendency to create Obstacle in their responses under frustrating situations has been noted more among the girls who reside with the working mothers and this too at age 13 which refers to the onset of puberty. Such tendency has not been noted among the girls who reside with non-working mothers. This shows indirectly that some type of frustration is comparatively more present among the girls who reside with the working mothes. This is why they display more of Obstacle Dominance.

B. EGO DEFENCE

The table below gives statistics calculated on the basis of the scores obtained by the gorups of girls on Ego Defence.

Table 64: Statistics for Groups on Ego Defence

Groups		Girls-Working Mothers			Girls-Non Working Mothers		
		N	Mean	S.D.	N	Mean	S.D.
Pre-pubertal	9	50	13.00	1.15	50	12.38	2.83
Pre-pubertal	11	50	11.60	3.02	50	11.36	2.93
Pubertal	13	50	10.18	2.65	50	11.90	1.34

Table 65 : Analysis of Variance for Groups on Ego Defence

Source of variation	df	Sums of Squares	Mean Square (Variance)	F
Between Means	5	231.03	46.202	
Within Groups	294	1756.88	5.9758	7.73**

** Significant at 0.01 level.

* Significant at 0.05 level.

The F-ratio obtained here is significant at 0.01 level. This shows that mean differences are significant. In order to find out which of the means differ significantly from each other, the t values were calculated and these have been reported below in the table.

Table 66: Comparisons of Groups on Ego Defence

	Groups	Age	N	Mean	S.D.	t Value
A	Girls Working Mothers	9	50	13.00	1.15	AB =3.11**
B	Girls Working Mothers	11	50	11.60	3.02	AC=7.05**
C	Girls Working Mothers	13	50	10.18	2.65	BC=2.49**
D	Girls Non-Working Mothers	9	50	12.38	2.83	DE=1.79
E	Girls Non-Working Mothers	11	50	11.36	2.93	DF=1.09
F	Girls Non-Working Mothers	13	50	11.90	1.34	EF=1.17
	**Significant at 0.01 level * Significant at 0.05 level					AD=1.44 BE=0.41 CF=4.09**

Analysis and Interpretation

In the above mentioned table four t values are significant. Of these one is significant at 0.05 level and three are significant at 0.01 level. This helps to interpret as follows.

1. The vartical comparisons of the means representing the preformance of the girls who reside with the working mothers show that with the rise in age the Ego Defence weakens significantly. As compared to the strength of ego defence at the age 9, the strength of ego defence at age 11 and at age 13 has decreased.
2. On the other hand the three means at these three levels do not differ significantly in the case of girls who reside with the non-working mothers. This shows that at all the developmental stages their level of ego defence more or less remains the same.
3. The agewise differences somehow do not disclose any significant differences between the girls of working mothers and of non-working mothers at age 9 and at age 11. But at age 13 the mean for the girls of non-working mothers is comparatively so high that it helps to conclude that the ego defence of the girls of non-working mothers is high as compared to those who reside with the working mothers.

The above conclusions indirectly tell that the absence of mothers from home and their involvement in job weakens the ego of their daughters. Whereas the control and gudiance of non-working mothers gives an opportunity to their daughters to develop proper ego strength for defending their Ego in frustrating situations.

C. NEED PERSISTANCE

The table below gives statistics derived on the basis of the scores obtained by the various groups of girls on Need Persistance:

Table 67: Statistics for Groups on Need Persistance

Groups		Girls-Working Mothers			Girls-Non Working Mothers		
		N	Mean	S.D.	N	Mean	S.D.
Pre-pubertal	9	50	6.94	3.16	50	7.44	2.79
Pre-pubertal	11	50	8.56	3.07	50	8.66	2.88
Pubertal	13	50	8.72	2.42	50	8.40	2.97

Table 68: Analyss of Variance for Groups on Need Persistance

Source of variation	df	Sums of Squares	Mean Square (Variance)	F
Between Means	5	138.92	27.784	
Within Groups	294	2458.1487	8.36	3.32**

** Significant at 0.01 level.

* Significant at 0.05 level.

The F-ratio is significant at 0.01 level. This tells that some of the groups of girls differ significatly in their performance from each other on this variable of study.

To find out, which of the groups differ in this regard, the t values were calculated and they have been reported below in the table.

Table 69: Comparisons of Groups on Need Persistance

	Groups	Age	N	Mean	S.D.	t Value
A	Girls Working Mothers	9	50	6.94	3.16	AB =1.84
B	Girls Working Mothers	11	50	8.56	3.07	AC=3.17**
C	Girls Working Mothers	13	50	8.72	2.42	BC=0.29
D	Girls Non-Working Mothers	9	50	7.44	2.79	DE=2.14**
E	Girls Non-Working Mothers	11	50	8.66	2.88	DF=1.65
F	Girls Non-Working Mothers	13	50	8.40	2.97	EF=0.45
	**Significant at 0.01 level * Significant at 0.05 level					AD=0.85 BE=0.16 CF=0.59

Analysis and Interpretaion

The table above reports only two t values as significient, one at 0.05 level and the other at 0.01 level. This helps to conclude as follows.

1. In the case of girls residing with the working mothers, the means obtained for the groups aged 9 and for the group aged 13 differ significatly from each other. This shows that the level of Need Persistance among these girls remains more or less the same at age 9 and at age 11, but by the time they attain the age of 13 the level of Need Persistance goes up significantly.
2. On the other hand the situation is bit different in the case of girls residing with non-working mothers. The significent t value refering to the differences of the means for goups aged 9 and aged 11 reflect that by the time the girls attain the age of 11, Need Persistance significantly increases among them and further it remains up to the same level even at age 13.
3. The agewise differences of the means obtained for the girls of working and non-working mothers do not report any significant differences in their performance on Need Persistance. At all the three age levels, Need Persistance is more or less equally present among both the groups of girls. This helps to conclude that probabely Need Persistance and the tandency to expect solutions from someone is present among the girls of both the groups at higher stages of development because somehow their needs remain unfulfilled.

D. EXTRAPUNITIVENESS

The table below gives statistics derived on the basis of the scores obtained by the various groups of girls on Extrapunitiveness.

Table 70: Statistics for Groups on Extrapunitiveness

Groups		Girls-Working Mothers			Girls-Non Working Mothers		
		N	Mean	S.D.	N	Mean	S.D.
Pre-pubertal	9	50	13.02	3.31	50	13.98	3.54
Pre-pubertal	11	50	10.44	3.84	50	10.40	3.19
Pubertal	13	50	10.70	3.25	50	9.04	3.44

Table 71: Analysis of Variance for Groups on Extrapunitiveness

Source of variation	df	Sums of Squares	Mean Square (Variance)	F
Between Means	5	857.50	171.50	
Within Groups	294	3469.4695	11.8009	14.53**

** Significant at 0.01 level.
* Significant at 0.05 level.

The F-ratio obtained here is very highly significant at 0.01 level. This shows that various groups significantly differ on this variable. To find out which of the groups differ in this connection t values were calculated and they have been presented below in the table.

Talbe 72: Comparisons of Goups on Extrapunitiveness

	Groups	Age	N	Mean	S.D.	t Value
A	Girls Working Mothers	9	50	13.02	3.31	AB =3.58**
B	Girls Working Mothers	11	50	10.44	3.84	AC=3.52**
C	Girls Working Mothers	13	50	10.70	3.25	BC=0.37
D	Girls Non-Working Mothers	9	50	13.98	3.54	DE=5.26**
E	Girls Non-Working Mothers	11	50	10.40	3.19	DF=7.05**
F	Girls Non-Working Mothers	13	50	9.04	3.44	EF=2.06*
	**Significant at 0.01 level					AD=1.41
	* Significant at 0.05 level					BE=0.06
						CF=2.76**

Analysis and Interpretaion

In the above mentioned table six t values are significant one at 0.05 level and five and 0.01 level. This helps to interpret as follows :

1. The vertical comparisons of the means obtained at the different age groups for the girls residing with working mothers show that with the rise in age the tendency of Extrapunitiveness has significantly gone down upto the age 11. Since the two means for age 11 and age 13 do not differ significatly it seems that the decreased level of Extrapunitiveness is maintained further upto the age of 13.
2. In the case of girls resing with non-working mothers the decrease in Extrapunitiveness is also noted from age 9 to age 11, and then again from the age 11 to age 13. This shows that in the case of these girls the tendency of Extrapunitiveness is continuously more decreasing with rise in age.
3. The agewise comparisons show that at age 9 and also at age 11 Extrapunitiveness is more or less present in both the groups of girls at the equal level. But at age 13 this tendency comparatively has been displayed more by the girls residing with working mothers.

The study shows that in the beginning both the groups of girls have displayed more or less equal tendency of Extrapunitiveness but with rise in age this tendency of Extrapunitiveness, in other words tendency to throw blame on others or on someone in the environment is decreasing more comparatively among the girls residing with non-working mother. This may be for the reason that the girls residing with non-working mothers probabely might be facing less frustration than those who reside with the working mothers.

E. INTROPUNITIVENESS

The table below gives statistics derived on the basis of the scores achieved by the different groups of girls on Intropunitiveness.

Table 73: Statistics for Groups of Intropunitiveness

Groups		Girls-Working Mothers			Girls-Non Working Mothers		
		N	Mean	S.D.	N	Mean	S.D.
Pre-pubertal	9	50	4.56	1.88	50	4.54	1.66
Pre-pubertal	11	50	5.64	1.76	50	5.48	1.46
Pubertal	13	50	5.92	1.63	50	5.88	1.76

Table 74: Analysis of Variance for Groups on Intropunitiveness

Source of variation	df	Sums of Squares	Mean Square (Variance)	F
Between Means	5	99.30	19.86	
Within Groups	294	846.41	2.87	6.81**

** Significant at 0.01 level.
* Significant at 0.05 level.

The F-ratio obtained here is highly significant at 0.01 level. This shows that the different means refering to the performances of the different groups of girls differ significantly on this variable. To finc out where such differences occur, t values were calculated and they have been presented below in the table.

Table 75 : Comparisons of Groups on Intropunitiveness

	Groups	Age	N	Mean	S.D.	t Value
A	Girls Working Mothers	9	50	4.56	1.88	AB =3.00**
B	Girls Working Mothers	11	50	5.64	1.76	AC=3.02**
C	Girls Working Mothers	13	50	5.92	1.63	BC=0.80
D	Girls Non-Working Mothers	9	50	4.54	1.66	DE=3.03**
E	Girls Non-Working Mothers	11	50	5.48	1.46	DF=3.94**
F	Girls Non-Working Mothers	13	50	5.88	1.76	EF=1.25
						AD=0.05
						BE=0.50
						CF=0.12

**Significant at 0.01 level
* Significant at 0.05 level

Analysis and Interpretaion

The table above gives four t values as significant. All these are significant at 0.01 level. These help to conclude as follows :

1. The vertical comparisons of the means obtained for the three groups of girls residing with the working mothers show that with the rise in age the tendency of Intropuntiveness, in other words the tendency to accept blame, has increased. But, since the two means obtained for age 11 and age 13 do not differ significantly it can be interpreted that the increased tendency of Intropunitiveness is maintained further even at the age of 13.
2. The vertical comparisons of the means for the girls residing with non-working mothers also disclose similar facts. In other words the tendency of intropunitiveness increases among these girls also by the time they atttain the age of 11. Then further it is maintained even at the age of 13.
3. The agewise comparisons do not give any significant results. Since at all age levels the means for the two groups of girls do not differ significantly, it can be said that practically at all age level, Intropunitiveness has been displayed by them at the same level.

This shows that under both the environmental circumstances the tendency of Intropunitiveness increases among the girls with the rise in age, and under both the conditions the girls attempt to maintain this tendency of accepting blame, if at all such a situation arises.

F. IMPUNITIVENESS

The table below gives statistics derived on the basis of the scores obtained by the girls on Impunitiveness.

Table 76: Statistics for Groups on Impunitiveness

Groups		Girls-Working Mothers			Girls-Non Working Mothers		
		N	Mean	S.D.	N	Mean	S.D.
Pre-pubertal	9	50	6.42	3.29	50	5.44	2.78
Pre-pubertal	11	50	7.92	3.04	50	8.12	2.71
Pubertal	13	50	7.38	2.95	50	9.08	2.84

Table 77: Analysis of Variance for Groups on Impunitiveness

Source of variation	df	Sums of Squares	Mean Square (Variance)	F
Between Means	5	420.67	84.134	
Within Groups	294	2543.4087	8.65	9.72**

** Significant at 0.01 level.
* Significant at 0.05 level.

The F-ratio obtained here on the basis of Analysis of Variance is significant at 0.01 level, refering to the fact that some groups differ significantly in their performance on this variable of study.

To find out where such differences occur, t values were calculated and they have been reported below.

Table 78. Comparisons of Groups on Impunitiveness

	Groups	Age	N	Mean	S.D.	t Value
A	Girls Working Mothers	9	50	6.42	3.29	AB =2.38*
B	Girls Working Mothers	11	50	7.92	3.04	AC=1.55
C	Girls Working Mothers	13	50	7.38	2.95	BC=0.90
D	Girls Non-Working Mothers	9	50	5.44	2.78	DE=4.87**
E	Girls Non-Working Mothers	11	50	8.12	2.71	DF=6.50**
F	Girls Non-Working Mothers	13	50	9.08	2.84	EF=1.71
						AD=1.61
						BE=0.24
						CF=2.93**

**Significant at 0.01 level
* Significant at 0.05 level

INTERPRETATION

The table above gives four t values as significant, one at 0.05 level and three at 0.01 level. The facts may be analyzed as follows :

1. The vartical comparisons of the means for girls residing with the working mothers show that the two means obtained for age 9

and age 11 differ significantly. This shows that with rise in age, the girls here have displayed the tendency of impunitivenss more at age 11, but since the two means for age 11 and 13 do not differ, it can be said that at both age levely this tendency is maintained at equal level.

2. The vertical comparisons of the means for the girls residing with the non-working mothers practically also disclose the same phenomenon. Here too the means obtained for age 11 and for age 13 are significantly high as compared to the means for age 9, this shows that among these girls also the tendency of Impunitiveness significantly increases by the time they attain the age of 11 and then further it is maintained at the same level even at the age 13.
3. The agewise comparisons give no significant results for age 9 and 11. At the age of 13 the significant differences of the two means disclose that tendency of impunitiveness has been displayed more significantly by the girls residing with the non-working mothers.

The tendency of Impunitiveness have been found increasing among both the groups of girls with the rise in age. With the onset of puberty and entry into the adolescence period this seems to be a normal phenomenon. But since it is found more among the girls residing with non-working mothers, it may be because comparatively less fear is dominant among them. Whereas on the other hand, the girls residing with the working mothers may not dare more to evade blame under the frustrating situations.

Comparisons of Girls Residing with Working and Non-Working Mothers

(Reactions to Frustration)

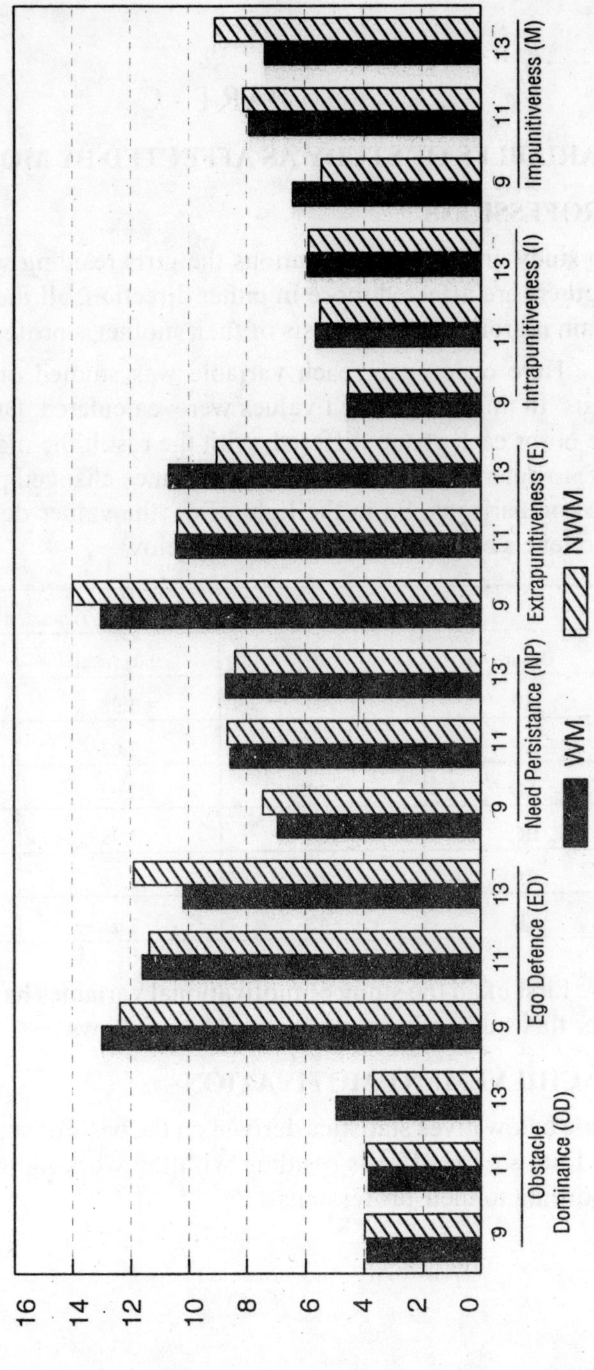

PART - C

VARIABLES OF STUDY AS AFFECTED BY MOTHER'S PROFESSIONS

To study under which situations the girls residing with the working mothers are affected more in either direction, all the girls were once again regrouped on the basis of their mother's professions.

Here once again each variable was studied on a comparative basis. In this study only t values were calculated. Due to regrouping the N for each group differed, with the result the digrees of freedom (df) to determine the levels of significance changed practically for all the comparisons. So in the light of df the values determined for the two levels of significance are given below.

		Tabulated Values	
Groups	df	0.05 level	0.01 level
AB	104	1.98	2.63
AC	47	2.02	2.69
AD	39	2.02	2.71
BC	107	1.98	2.63
BD	99	1.98	2.63
CD	42	2.02	2.71

First of all the study of motivational variables has been made and after this study of personality variables follows :

1. ACHIEVEMENT MOTIVATION

Table below gives statistics derived on the basis of scores obtained by the four groups of girls residing with the working mothers grouped according to their professions.

Table 79: Comparisons of girls Based on Mother's Profession (Achievement Motivation)

	Mother's Profession	N	Mean	S.D.	t Value
A	Medical	23	50.83	3.47	AB = 0.95
B	Teaching	83	51.86	4.76	AC = 0.50
C	Office Jobs	26	51.38	4.05	AD = 1.39
D	Self Employment	18	49.11	4.53	BC = 0.48
	** Significant at 0.01 level				BD = 2.23*
	* Significant at 0.05 level				CD = 1.72

Analysis and Interpretaion

In the table only one t value is significant. This is significant at 0.05 level. This shows that the two means referring to the performances of the girls of group B and D differs significantly from each other, since the mean obtained for the group D is significantly low, it can be interpreted that achievement motivation is comparatively high among the girls who are residing with the working mothers employed in the teaching profession. On the other hand it is low among the girls residing with the mothers self employed.

Since the means obtained for the groups A,B and C do not differ significantly from each other, it is clear that the achievement motivation among the girls residing with the mothers working in office jobs, as teachers or in medical profession is more or less same.

2. MANIFEST ANXIETY

The table below gives statistics obtained on the basis of scores secured by the four groups of girls residing with the working mothers grouped in the light of their profession.

Table 80: Comparisons of Girls Based on Mother's Profession (Manifest Anxiety)

	Mother's Profession	N	Mean	S.D.	t Value
A	Medical	23	23.83	7.33	AB = 0.29
B	Teaching	83	24.46	9.45	AC = 0.88
C	Office Jobs	26	25.85	8.36	AD = 0.07
D	Self Employment	18	24.00	7.69	BC = 0.69
	** Significant at 0.01 level				BD = 0.19
	* Significant at 0.05 level				CD = 0.74

Analysis and Interpretation

The above mentioned table does not report any t value as significant. This makes it clear that the means obtained on this variable of study by the whole group of girls do not differ significantly from each other. This helps to interpret that the level of anxiety manifested by the four groups of girls is more or less the same. One can interpret on this basis that the development of anxiety among the girls is not influenced by the nature of the profession joined by the mohter.

3. SELF CONCEPT

The table below provides statistics obtained on the basis of scores secured by the four groups of girls residing with the working mothers grouped here in the light of their profession.

Table 81: Comparisons of Girls Based on Mother's Profession (Self Concept)

	Mother's Profession	N	Mean	S.D.	t Value
A	Medical	23	34.83	5.52	AB = 1.41
B	Teaching	83	32.01	8.51	AC = 1.17
C	Office Jobs	26	32.50	7.90	AD = 1.50
D	Self Employment	18	32.00	6.73	BC = 0.27
	** Significant at 0.01 level				BD = 0.01
	* Significant at 0.05 level				CD = 0.22

Analysis and Interpretation

None of the t values given in the above table is significant. This refers to the fact that all the means refering to the performances of the four groups of girls on this variable do not differ significantly from each other. This helps to observe that the development of self concept among girls beloning to four groups mentioned here is more or less on the same lines.

4. MATURITY

(a) INTELLECTUAL MATURITY

The table below gives statistics derived on the basis of scores obtained by four groups of girls residing with the working mothers grouped seperately on the basis of the professions.

Talbe 82: Comparisons of Girls Based on Mother's Profession (Intellectual Maturity)

	Mother's Profession	N	Mean	S.D.	t Value
A	Medical	23	36.52	5.35	AB = 0.90
B	Teaching	83	37.81	6.16	AC = 0.86
C	Office Jobs	26	35.03	6.45	AD = 1.65
D	Self Employment	18	39.33	5.70	BC = 2.02*
	** Significant at 0.01 level				BD = 0.96
	* Significant at 0.05 level				CD = 2.26*

Analysis and Interpretation

In the table given above, two t values are significant. Both these are significant at 0.05 level. In both these cases, the mean obtained for the girls of group C is significantly low as compared to the means obtained for the girls of groups B and D. It is also seen that the means obtained for the group A, B and D do not differ significantly.

This shows that among the three groups of girls who are residing with the mothers self employed, or employed in the medical or teaching profession the intellectual maturity is more or less at the same level. On the other hand, the group of girls residng with the mothers busy in office jobs have displayed low level of intellectual maturity. This helps to interpret that the development of intellectual maturity is affected by the nature of the profession adopted by the mother.

(b) EMOTIONAL MATURITY

The table below provides statistics derived on the basis of the scores obtained by the four groups of girls residing with the working mothers, grouped on the basis of the professions.

Talbe 83: Comparisons of Girls Based on Mother's Profession (Emotional Maturity)

	Mother's Profession	N	Mean	S.D.	t Value
A	Medical	23	35.48	7.54	AB = 0.56
B	Teaching	83	36.33	6.38	AC = 1.12
C	Office Jobs	26	33.00	7.70	AD = 0.95
D	Self Employment	18	37.56	6.46	BC = 2.27*
	** Significant at 0.01 level				BD = 0.74
	* Significant at 0.05 level				CD = 2.04*

Analysis and Interpretation

The table reports only two t values as significant. Both these are significant at 0.05 level. Here, the comparison of the means obtained by the groups of girls B, C and D shows that the means obtained by the girls of the group C is significanty low. On the other hand the three means obtained for groups A,B and D are not different significantly.

This shows that the girls of group C residing with the mother doing office jobs have displayed low level of emotional maturity. On the other hand the level of emotional maturity shown by the girls residing with mother self employed or working as teachers is comparatively better.

It is also noted that the girls residing with mothers who are working as teachers or employed in medical profession or self employed have practically exhibited more or less same level of emotional maturity. Here too it is clear that the development of emotional maturity among girls is positively influenced by the nature of mothers profession.

(c) SOCIAL MATURITY

The table below gives statistics derived on the basis of the score achieved by the four groups of girls residing with the working mothers grouped in the light of their professions.

Talbe 84: Comparisons of Girls Based on Mother's Profession (Social Maturity)

	Mother's Profession	N	Mean	S.D.	t Value
A	Medical	23	38.09	5.20	AB = 0.24
B	Teaching	83	38.45	6.38	AC = 0.71
C	Office Jobs	26	36.73	7.69	AD = 0.06
D	Self Employment	18	38.22	7.93	BC =1.16
	** Significant at 0.01 level				BD = 0.13
	* Significant at 0.05 level				CD = 0.62

Analysis and Interpretaion

In the above table none of the t value is significant. This shows that the four means referring to the level of social maturity of the four groups of girls, do not differ significantly from each other.

This helps to interpret that the girls of the four groups have practically exhibited same level of social maturity. In other words this shows that the development of social maturity is not affected by the mother's profession in either direction.

PERSONALITY FACTOR

FACTOR A - Reserved vs Warmhearted

The table below gives the statistics derived on the basis of the scores obtaind by the four groups of girls grouped according to their mothers professions.

Table 85: Comparisons of Girls Based on Mother's Profession

(FACTOR A - Reserved : Warmhearted)

	Mother's Profession	N	Mean	S.D.	t Value
A	Medical	23	6.57	1.58	AB = 0.08
B	Teaching	83	6.54	1.42	AC = 1.06
C	Office Jobs	26	6.08	1.672	AD = 1.09
D	Self Employment	18	7.08	1.41	BC = 1.09
	** Significant at 0.01 level				BD = 1.46
	* Significant at 0.05 level				CD = 2.08*

Analysis and Interpretation

In the above mentioned table only one t value is significant. This t value is significant at 0.05 level. It is related with two means obtained for groups C and D. In this case the mean for group D is significantly and comparatively high. It may be mentioned here that practically all the four means are slightly bending towards high score description referring to the phenomenonof warm heartedness. This shows that whereas all the girls are warmhearted and participating, the girls residing with the mothers self employed are significantly more warm hearted, participating and outgoing.

FACTOR B - Dull vs Bright

The table below gives statistics derived on the basis of the scores achieved by the four groups of the girls on this variable.

Table 86: Comparisons of Girls Based on Mother's Profession

(FACTOR B - Dull : Bright)

	Mother's Profession	N	Mean	S.D.	t Value
A	Medical	23	5.61	1.50	AB = 1.39
B	Teaching	83	5.08	1.60	AC = 0.24
C	Office Jobs	26	5.50	1.60	AD = 1.66
D	Self Employment	18	4.88	1.68	BC = 1.24
	** Significant at 0.01 level				BD = 0.50
	* Significant at 0.05 level				CD = 1.24

Analysis and Interpretation

In above mentioned table, no t value is significant. This shows that the four means mentioned above in the table and referring to the inteilectual performances of the four groups of girls do not differ significantly from each other. This further helps to analyse and interpret that practically all the girls belonging to the four groups possess equal intellectual ability.

FACTOR C - Affected by feelings vs Emotionally stable

The table below provides statistics calculated on the basis of the scores secured by the four groups of the girls grouped according to the mothers professions.

Table 87: Comparisons of Girls Based on Mother's Profession

(FACTOR C - Affected by feelings : Emotionally stable)

	Mother's Profession	N	Mean	S.D.	t Value
A	Medical	23	7.05	2.09	AB = 1.46
B	Teaching	83	6.45	1.60	AC = 1.56
C	Office Jobs	26	6.19	1.73	AD = 0.49
D	Self Employment	18	7.33	1.49	BC = 0.72
	** Significant at 0.01 level				BD = 2.15*
	* Significant at 0.05 level				CD = 2.24*

Analysis and Interpretation

In this table two t values are significant.Both these values are related with groups B and D, and C and D. In both these cases the mean obtained by the girls of group D is significantly and comparatively high. Since the means above refers slightly to high score description, it can be said that the girls residing with the mothers self employed are more emotionaly stable. Whereas the girls residing with the mothers doing office jobs and those in teaching professions are comparatively less emotionally stable. Since the two means for groups A and D do not differ significantly and are close to each other, it can be interpreted that the girls residing with mothers engageed in medical profession are also emotinally stable.

FACTOR D - Phlegmatic vs Excitable

This table presents statistics derived on the basis of the scores obtained on this factor by the four groups of girls grouped according to their mothers professions.

Table 88: Comparisons of Girls Based on Mother's Profession

(FACTOR D - Phlegmatic : Excitable)

	Mother's Profession	N	Mean	S.D.	t Value
A	Medical	23	3.30	1.71	AB = 0.20
B	Teaching	83	3.22	1.61	AC = 1.07
C	Office Jobs	26	3.77	1.67	AD = 1.59
D	Self Employment	18	3.11	2.31	BC = 1.53
	** Significant at 0.01 level				BD = 0.24
	* Significant at 0.05 level				CD = 1.08

Analysis and Interpretation

None of the t value is significant in this table. This refers to the fact that the means mentioned therein do not differ significantly from each other. This further helps to interpret that the performances of the four groups of girls on this factor D are more or less equal. Because the scores in all the four cases have inclination towards low score description, it is clear that practically all the girls are phlegmatic in nature, rather not very much impatient.

FACTOR E - Obedient vs Dominant

The table below gives statistics calculated on the basis of the scores obtained on factor E by the four groups of girls residing with their mothers grouped in the light of their professions.

Table 89: Comparisons of Girls Based on Mother's Profession

(FACTOR E - Obedient : Dominant)

	Mother's Profession	N	Mean	S.D.	t Value
A	Medical	23	3.35	1.71	AB = 0.15
B	Teaching	83	3.41	1.61	AC = 0.53
C	Office Jobs	26	3.58	1.28	AD = 0.84
D	Self Employment	18	3.78	1.55	BC = 0.50
					BD = 0.80
					CD = 0.47

** Significant at 0.01 level
* Significant at 0.05 level

Analysis and Interpretation

In this table none of the t value is significant, referring to the fact that all the means presented above in the table do not differ significantly from each other. This shows that the performances of the four groups of girls on factor E is more or less displayed same type of trait among all the girls. In other words it can be said that because of low score description among the means, more or less all the groups of girls are comparatively obedient and accomodating in nature.

FACTOR F - Sober vs Enthusiastic

This table gives statistics derived on the basis of the scores obtained on factor F by the four groups of girls grouped in the light of their mothers professions.

Table 90: Comparisons of Girls Based on Mother's Profession

(FACTOR F - Sober : Enthusiastic)

	Mother's Profession	N	Mean	S.D.	t Value
A	Medical	23	5.26	1.85	AB = 2.68**
B	Teaching	83	4.24	1.53	AC = 0.68
C	Office Jobs	26	4.88	1.99	AD = 0.98
D	Self Employment	18	4.72	1.66	BC = 1.78
					BD = 1.14
					CD = 0.28

** Significant at 0.01 level
* Significant at 0.05 level

Analysis and Interpretation

In the above mentioned table only one t value is significant. This t value is significant at 0.01 level and refers to significant high mean difference among the two means for groups A and B.

This shows that the girls residing with the mothers engaged in medical profession have a leaning towards enthusiasm and becoming frank and expressive. On the other hand the girls residing with the mothers employed in teaching profession are sober and serious. Since the other two means for group C and D do not differ significantly as compared to the mean for group B, it can be said that the girls residing with the mothers self employed and doing office jobs display soberity in their behaviour.

FACTOR G - Expedient vs Conscientious

The table mentioned below describes the statistics calculated on the basis of the score on factor G by the four groups of girls grouped according to their mothers professions.

Table 91: Comparisons of Girls Based on Mother's Profession

(FACTOR G - Expedient : Conscientious)

	Mother's Profession	N	Mean	S.D.	t Value
A	Medical	23	7.26	2.00	AB = 0.41
B	Teaching	83	7.42	1.53	AC = 1.41
C	Office Jobs	26	6.50	1.71	AD = 0.07
D	Self Employment	18	7.22	1.90	BC = 2.63**
					BD = 0.49
					CD = 1.31

** Significant at 0.01 level
* Significant at 0.05 level

Analysis and Interpretation

In this table only one t value is significant . This t value is significant at 0.01 level, referring to the phenomenon that the two means obtained for groups B and C differ quite significantly from each other. Here the mean obtained for the girls residing with mothers engaged in teaching profession is high. This shows that these girls are more conscientious and possess strong super ego. Comparatively the girls residing with the mothers doing office jobs are less conscientious.

The means obtained for group A, B and D do not differ significantly and are rather very close to each other. This shows that the girls residing with mothers self employed or with mothers engaged in teaching and medical professions are also quite conscientious and rule-bound.

FACTOR H - Shy vs Venturesome

In the table below, the statistics has been derived on the basis of the scores obtained on factor H by the four groups of girls grouped further on the basis of mothers professions.

Table 92: Comparisons of Girls Based on Mother's Profession

(FACTOR H - Shy : Venturesome)

	Mother's Profession	N	Mean	S.D.	t Value
A	Medical	23	6.09	1.38	AB = 0.69
B	Teaching	83	6.34	1.56	AC = 1.21
C	Office Jobs	26	5.62	1.33	AD = 0.19
D	Self Employment	18	6.00	1.76	BC = 2.18*
	** Significant at 0.01 level				BD = 0.82
	* Significant at 0.05 level				CD = 0.81

Analysis and Interpretation

In this table only one t value is significant. The level of significance here is 0.05 level. This refers to the fact that the means obtained for group B and C differ significantly from each other. Since the mean here is high for the girls of group B, it can be said that the girls residing with the mothers busy in teaching profession are slightly more venturesome and socially bold than the girls residing with the mothers doing office jobs. Since the other two means for group A and D are also very close to mean for group B, it can be interpreted that the girls residing with mothers self employed or engaged in medical profession are also socially bold and venturesome.

FACTOR I - Toughminded vs Tenderminded

The table below gives statistics derived on the basis of the scores obtained on this factor by the four groups of girls grouped according to mothers professions.

Table 93: Comparisons of Girls Based on Mother's Profession

(FACTOR I - Toughminded : Tenderminded)

	Mother's Profession	N	Mean	S.D.	t Value
A	Medical	23	4.35	1.13	AB = 3.12**
B	Teaching	83	5.35	1.38	AC = 0.71
C	Office Jobs	26	4.62	1.44	AD = 2.06*
D	Self Employment	18	5.32	1.45	BC = 2.35*
	** Significant at 0.01 level				BD = 0.08
	* Significant at 0.05 level				CD = 1.56

Analysis and Interpretation

In this table three t values are significant. Two are significant at 0.05 level and one at 0.01 level. One tells about the difference among the means for group A and B, second one about the differences between the means for groups A and D, and the third about the differences between groups B and C. All these tell that the girls with mothers engaged in teaching profession and with mothers self employed are moving towards tendermindedness. Whereas the girls residing with mothers in medical profession and doing office jobs are slightly tough minded.

FACTOR J - Zestful vs Circumspect Individualism

The table below gives statistics derived on the basis of the scores obtained on factor J by the four groups of girls grouped according to mothers professions.

Table 94: Comparisons of Girls Based on Mother's Profession

(FACTOR J - Zestful : Circumspect)

	Mother's Profession	N	Mean	S.D.	t Value
A	Medical	23	4.57	1.44	AB = 0.28
B	Teaching	83	4.46	1.67	AC = 3.08**
C	Office Jobs	26	5.77	1.28	AD = 0.98
D	Self Employment	18	4.11	1.59	BC = 3.85**
	** Significant at 0.01 level				BD = 0.81
	* Significant at 0.05 level				CD = 3.77**

Analysis and Interpretation

This table gives three t values as significant. All these t values are significant at 0.01 level. This tells that comparatively in all these three cases, the mean obtained for group C is significantly much higher than the means for groups A, B and D. This refers to the fact that girls residing with the mothers doing office jobs are more individually strict and guarded in their actions, whereas the girls residing with mothers engaged in medical and teaching professions or self employed are vigorous, liking group actions.

FACTOR N - Forthright vs Shrewd

The table below mentions statistics derived on the basis of scores obtained on factor N by the four groups of girls grouped as follows.

Table 95: Comparisons of Girls Based on Mother's Profession

(FACTOR N - Forthright : Shrewd)

	Mother's Profession	N	Mean	S.D.	t Value
A	Medical	23	3.52	1.56	AB = 0.71
B	Teaching	83	3.25	1.60	AC = 0.22
C	Office Jobs	26	3.42	1.57	AD = 1.31
D	Self Employment	18	2.89	1.52	BC = 0.49
	** Significant at 0.01 level				BD = 0.88
	* Significant at 0.05 level				CD = 1.10

Analysis and Interpretation

None of the t value is significant in this table. This shows that the four means mentioned above in the table do not differ significantly from each other. Since all the scores are referring to low score description, this implies that practically the girls of all the four groups are more forthright and natural in their behaviour, more or less equally.

FACTOR O - Self Assured vs Guilt Prone

The table below presents statistics derived on the basis of the scores obtained on factor O by the four groups of girls grouped as under.

Table 96: Comparisons of Girls Based on Mother's Profession

(FACTOR O - Self Assured : Guilt Prone)

	Mother's Profession	N	Mean	S.D.	t Value
A	Medical	23	3.83	1.58	AB = 0.40
B	Teaching	83	3.65	1.95	AC = 0.04
C	Office Jobs	26	3.81	2.00	AD = 1.50
D	Self Employment	18	3.11	1.52	BC = 0.37
					BD = 1.10
					CD = 1.25

** Significant at 0.01 level
* Significant at 0.05 level

Analysis and Interpretation

In the table above none of the t value is significant. This shows that the means given above in the table do not differ significantly, referring to the fact that four groups of girls possess this trait more or less equally and display the same at equal level. This further helps to say that because of low score description practically all the girls are self assured and feel confident and secured, more or less equally.

FACTOR Q3 - Undisciplined Self vs Controlled

The table below gives statistics derived on the basis of the scores obtained on factor Q3 by the four groups of girls grouped in the light of their mothers professions.

Table 97: Comparisons of Girls Based on Mother's Profession

(FACTOR Q3 - Undisciplined Self: Controlled)

	Mother's Profession	N	Mean	S.D.	t Value
A	Medical	23	6.04	2.33	AB = 2.93*
B	Teaching	83	7.39	1.80	AC = 1.24
C	Office Jobs	26	6.81	1.98	AD = 1.57
D	Self Employment	18	7.11	2.04	BC = 1.41
	** Significant at 0.01 level				BD = 0.58
	* Significant at 0.05 level				CD = 0.48

Analysis and Interpretation

In the table described here only one t value is significant. The level of significance here is 0.05. This value is connected with the two means for groups A and B. Here comparatively the mean obtained for group B is significantly high. Since all the means obtained here refers to high score description, it can be said that the girls residing with the mothers employed in teaching are more controlled and socially precise than those who are residing with mothers engaged in medical profession.

On the other hand it is also noted that the two means for group A and C are quite close to each other. This shows that the girls residing with the mothers engaged in medical professions and with mothers doing office jobs are practically a bit less controlled. Whereas the two means for group B and D, being close to each other helped to interpret that the girls residing with mothers self employed and with mothers working as teachers are comparatively more controlled and at equal level.

FACTOR Q4 - Relaxed vs Tense

The table below provides statistics derived on the basis of the scores obtained on factor Q4 by the four groups of girls grouped according to mothers professions.

Table 98: Comparisons of Girls Based on Mother's Profession

(FACTOR Q_4 - Relaxed : Tense)

	Mother's Profession	N	Mean	S.D.	t Value
A	Medical	23	3.57	2.12	AB = 1.17
B	Teaching	83	3.01	2.01	AC = 0.57
C	Office Jobs	26	3.92	2.09	AD = 0.94
D	Self Employment	18	3.04	2.24	BC = 2.02*
	** Significant at 0.01 level				BD = 0.13
	* Significant at 0.05 level				CD = 1.46

Analysis and Interpretation

In this table only one t value is significant. The level of significance here is 0.05. This discloses that the two means obtained for groups B and C differs significantly from each other. Here practically all the scores are referring to low score description. Therefore, it can be safely interpreted that the girls residing with mothers engaged in teaching profession are more relaxed and unfrustrated, whereas the girls residing with mothers doing office jobs are comparatively less relaxed.

The means obtained for group B and D are quite close. On the other hand the means obtained for group A and C are also quite close. On this basis, two points emerge. The girls residing with mothers self employed and with mothers working as teachers are comparatively more relaxed, and the girls residing with mothers doing office jobs and with mothers engaged in medical professions are slightly less relaxed.

REACTIONS TO FRUSTRATION

A. Obstacle Dominance

The table below gives statistics derived on the basis of scores achieved by the four groups of girls residing with the working mothers grouped here on the basis of professions.

Table 99: Comparisons of Girls Based on Mother's Profession

(Obstacle Dominance)

	Mother's Profession	N	Mean	S.D.	t Value
A	Medical	23	3.74	1.38	AB = 0.31
B	Teaching	83	3.84	1.32	AC = 2.03*
C	Office Jobs	26	4.55	1.41	AD = 1.23
D	Self Employment	18	4.28	1.45	BC = 2.37*
					BD = 1.26
					CD = 0.61

** Significant at 0.01 level
* Significant at 0.05 level

Analysis and Interpretation

In the table above only two t values are significant. Both these are significant at 0.05 level. This shows that the means obtained for the groups A and C, and for groups B and C differ significantly from each other. In both these cases the mean obtained for group C is significantly high. This exhibits that the girls whose mothers are engaged in office jobs have displayed a high tendency of obstacle dominance. On the other hand the means for group C and D do not differ significantly. This shows that the girls whose mothers are self employed also display high obstacle dominance. The insignificant t values for group A and B, reflects that the girls whose mothers are engaged in medical and teaching professions possess equal tendency of obstacle dominance, but comparatively lower than others.

B. Ego Defence

The table below gives the statistics based on the scores obtained by the four groups of girls residing with the working mothers grouped according to the professions they have adopted.

Table 100 : Comparisons of Girls Based on Mother's Profession

(Ego Defence)

	Mother's Profession	N	Mean	S.D.	t Value
A	Medical	23	12.99	2.77	AB = 1.03
B	Teaching	83	12.24	3.13	AC = 2.03*
C	Office Jobs	26	11.37	2.81	AD = 0.26
D	Self Employment	18	13.22	2.84	BC = 0.95
					BD = 1.13
					CD = 2.13*

** Significant at 0.01 level
* Significant at 0.05 level

Analysis and Interpretation

The table above gives only two t values as significant. Both these values are significant at 0.05 level. These t values are related with the groups A and C, and groups C and D. In both cases, the mean obtained by the girls of group C is significantly low in comparison to the means in group A and D. This shows that ego defence is weak in the case of the girls whose mothers are doing office jobs. Whereas in the case of the girls whose mothers are self employed and also in case of those whose mothers are serving in the medical profession, the ego predominates more, comparatively.

One thing more is noted. The means for group A, B and D do not differ significantly. This helps to interpret that the ego of the girls who reside with the mothers engaged in teaching profession is also comparatively quite strong.

C. NEED PERSISTANCE

The table below provids statistics derived on the basis of the scores achieved by the four groups of girls residing with their working mothers grouped further according to the professions they have joined.

Table 101: Comparisons of Girls Based on Mother's Profession

(Need Persistance)

	Mother's Profession	N	Mean	S.D.	t Value
A	Medical	23	7.52	2.45	AB = 0.87
B	Teaching	83	8.14	3.06	AC = 0.48
C	Office Jobs	26	7.88	2.73	AD = 1.20
D	Self Employment	18	6.50	3.08	BC = 0.40
					BD = 2.08*
					CD = 1.55

** Significant at 0.01 level
* Significant at 0.05 level

Analysis and Interpretation

The above table shows only one t value significant. This is signficant at 0.05 level. This t value is related with the two means for group B and D. Here, the mean obtained for the girls residing with the mothers self employed is significantly low whereas the mean for the girls whose mothers are working in the teaching professions is significantly high. This makes it very clear that need persistance is high among the girls where the mothers are working as teachers.

Since the means for the groups A, B and C do not differ significantly, it can be said that need persistance is visible in case of other two groups also, i.e. among the girls whose mothers are in medical profession and in office jobs.

D. Extrapunitiveness

The table below gives statistics derived on the basis of the scores obtained on this variable by the four groups of girls who are residing with their working mothers grouped into four professions as mentioned in the table.

Table 102: Comparisons of Girls Based on Mother's Profession

(Extrapunitiveness)

	Mother's Profession	N	Mean	S.D.	t Value
A	Medical	23	11.17	3.84	AB = 0.28
B	Teaching	83	10.90	4.12	AC = 0.02
C	Office Jobs	26	11.15	4.04	AD = 0.22
D	Self Employment	18	11.44	4.26	BC = 0.28
	** Significant at 0.01 level				BD = 0.50
	* Significant at 0.05 level				CD = 0.23

Analysis and Interpretation

In this table, no t value is significant. This shows that significant difference are not been reflected among the different means referring to the performance of the four groups of girls on the variable of extrapunitiveness. This shows that practically among all the girls, irrespective of their mothers professions the tendency to turn blame or hostility on some one in the environment is more or less equal.

E. Intropunitiveness

The table below provides statistics derived on the basis of scores obtained on this variable by the girls who reside with their working mothers grouped further according to the professions they have adopted.

Table 103: Comparisons of Girls Based on Mother's Profession

(Intropunitiveness)

	Mother's Profession	N	Mean	S.D.	t Value
A	Medical	23	5.39	1.86	AB = 0.17
B	Teaching	83	5.31	1.99	AC = 0.78
C	Office Jobs	26	5.77	1.55	AD = 0.91
D	Self Employment	18	4.89	1.69	BC = 1.09
	** Significant at 0.01 level				BD = 0.79
	* Significant at 0.05 level				CD = 1.80

Analysis and Interpretation

In this table not a single t value is significant at any level. This tells that the four means given above in the table and referring to the performances of the four groups of girls do not differ significantly from each other. This further tells that the tendency of intropunitiveness is more or less equal among all the four groups of girls without taking into account the professions their mothers have taken up. Practically all the girls possess the tendency of accepting blame under circumstances more or less equally.

F. Impunitiveness

The table below provides statstics calculated on the basis of the scores achieved by the four groups of girls residing with the mothers grouped in light of their profession.

Table 104: Comparisons of Girls Based on Mother's Profession

(Impunitiveness)

	Mother's Profession	N	Mean	S.D.	t Value
A	Medical	23	7.43	3.12	AB = 0.43
B	Teaching	83	7.75	3.08	AC = 0.36
C	Office Jobs	26	7.08	3.47	AD = 0.24
D	Self Employment	18	7.67	3.45	BC = 0.97
	** Significant at 0.01 level				BD = 0.11
	* Significant at 0.05 level				CD = 0.55

Analysis and Interpretation

None of the t value is significant here in the table. This tells that the means mentioned above in the table do not differ significantly in any way from each other. This tells that the tendency of impunitiveness or evading blame is practically equally possessed by all the girls grouped on the basis of mothers profesions.

PART - D

CASE STUDY

As mentioned in the earlier pages, 40 girls were subjected to case study-20 girls who were residing with the working mothers and 20 girls who were residing with the non -working mothers. In both the groups 10 girls were selected randomly from the prepurbertal groups and 10 from the pubertal groups. While interviewing the individual cases, an attempt was made to locate points more or less under the same variables of study which were selected for this reserch project. To be more specific, the idea was to locate actual sources of motivation for achievement, reasons for anxiety hurdles, if any in the development of personality and self concept, factors leading to immaturity, and reasons for frustration. Ultimately it was also thrashed out what are the merits and demarits of mother's employment.

The following table provides percentage in terms of girl's responses selected from both the major groups.

Table 105 : Case Study Schedule

No.	Variables Discussed	Girls with Working Mothers		Girls with Non-Working Mothers	
		20	%	20	%
1.	Sources of motivation for achievement				
	- Father	6	30	12	60
	- Mother	8	40	16	80
	- Siblings	10	50	4	20
	- Neighbours	6	30	-	-
	- Classmates	14	70	6	30
	- Relations	10	50	4	20

No.	Variables Discussed	Girls with Working Mothers		Girls with Non-Working Mothers	
		20	%	20	%
2.	Reasons for anxiety				
	- Insufficient income	8	40	14	70
	- Heavy courses of study	12	60	10	50
	- Poor physical development	5	25	6	30
	- Absence of mother's guidance	15	75	3	15
	- No help in home work	8	40	7	35
	- No solution of personel problems	16	80	4	20
	- Burden of household chores	16	80	3	15
	- High expectations of parents	15	75	12	60
3.	Development of self concept				
	- Poor achievement	10	50	14	70
	- Unfulfilled ambitions	6	30	14	70
	- Weak ego strength	4	20	14	70
	- Poor health guidance	8	40	2	10
	- Lack of home discussions	12	60	5	25
	- Unrealistic goals	14	70	3	15
	- Successive failure	4	20	5	25
4.	Maturity-Intellectual				
	- Lack of academic guidance	14	70	6	30
	- Less time for self study	16	80	8	40
	- Lack of academic discussions	15	75	14	70
	- Too much interference	4	20	16	80
	- Less time for viewing TV programmes	10	50	4	20
	Maturity - Emotional				
	- Tensions in home	14	70	6	30
	- Poor school achievement	8	40	13	65
	- Sibling rivalry	4	20	6	30
	- Aggression in home environment	3	15	3	15
	Maturity-Social				
	- Less time for social visits	15	75	6	30
	- Poor social circles	4	20	9	45
	- Missing social gatherings	14	70	2	10
	- Missing town programmes	10	50	7	35

No.	Variables Discussed	Girls with Working Mothers		Girls with Non-Working Mothers	
		20	%	20	%
5.	Reasons for frustration				
	- Unfulfilment of needs	5	25	15	75
	- More of home duties	16	80	2	10
	- Unrealistic demands of parents	16	80	4	20
	- Lack of recognition	4	20	12	60
	- Disturbances in studies	16	80	4	20
	- Use of defence mechanism(Like withdrawl, Repression, aggression, reaction formation)	14	70	10	50
6.	Obstacles in personality development				
	- No time for explorations	4	20	12	60
	- No time for adventures	6	30	11	55
	- Busy schedule of parents	15	75	4	20
	- Less time for indoor games	15	75	6	30
	- Less time for discussion on sports	12	60	4	20
	- Lack of communication with parents	14	70	3	15
	- Parental overprotection	3	15	12	60
	- Parental underprotection	12	60	2	10
	- Weak ego development	4	20	15	75
7.	Merits of mother's employment				
	- Economic uplift	14	70	4	20
	- Fulfilment of more needs	15	75	5	25
	- Status in society	12	60	10	50
	- Development of independence	16	80	4	20
	- Development of self confidence	17	85	5	25
	- Development of strong ego	16	80	4	20
8.	Demerits of mother's employment				
	- Lack of mother's guidance	16	80	2	10
	- Poor achievements of children	8	40	8	40
	- Poor hospitality to visitors	10	50	14	70
	- No discussion on family problems	14	70	4	20
	- Poor training of children	3	15	10	50
	- Poor home adjustments	10	50	10	50
	- Development of sibling rivalry	5	25	10	50
	- Less social relations	12	60	8	40

DISCUSSION

1. The girls residing with the working mothers have reported in majority that source of motivation for achievement is from siblings, classmates and relations. On the other hand the girls with non-working mothers in majority report that motivation for achivement comes from parents.

2. The girls residing with the working mothers have reported in majority that reasons for anxiety are heavy courses of study, absence of mother's guidance, unsolved personal problems, high expectations of parents and burdens of household chores. The reasons for anxiety reported by the girls residing with the non-working mothers are insufficient income, heavy courses of study and high expectations of parents.

3. The reasons as reported by the majority of girls residing with working mothers, in development of self concept are poor achievement, lack of home discussions and unrealistic goals. On the other hand, the points reported here by the girls residing with non-working mothers are poor achievement, unfulfilled ambitions and weak ego strength.

4. The girls with working mothers have reported that lack of academic gudiance, less time for viewing telivision programmes stand as obstacles for intellectual maturity. In the case of girls with non-working mothers lack of academic discussions and too much interference in work are obstacles for proper intellectual maturity.

   The girls with working mothers have reported that only tensions in home stand as an obstacte for proper emotional development. Whereas the girls with non-working mothers report that it is poor school achievement.

   The girls with working mothers have reported that the schedule of working mothers gives practically no time for social visits, social gathering and town programmes. The girls with the non-working mothers have reported that poor social circles stand in the way of proper social maturity

5. The reasons for frustration, as reported by the girls with working mothers are more of home duties, unrealistic demands of parents, disturbances in studies, which ultimately force them to

adopt certain defence mechanisms. The girls with non- working mothers have reported unfulfillment of needs and lack of recognition as reasons for frustration.

6. The girls residing with the working mothers have reported that improper personality development results from busy schedule of parents, less time for indoor games, less time for discussion on sports, lack of communication with parents and parental underprotection whereas the girls residing with the non-working mothers report that it is due to no time for adventures and explorations, parental overprotection and weak ego development.

7. Under merits of mother's employment the girls residing with the working mothers have reported economic uplift, fulfillment of more needs, status in society, development of independence, self confidence and strong ego. On the other hand, the girls residing with the non-working mothers report here only one factor and that is status in society.

8. Under demerits of mother's employment the girls residing with the working mothers report lack of mothers gudiance, poor hospitality to visitors, no discussion on family problems, less social relations and poor home adjustment. The girls residing gith the non-working mothers have reported here poor hospitality to visitors, poor training of children, poor home adjustment and development of sibling rivalry as some of the demerits of mother's employment.

Chapter - 4

Findings and Suggestions

This chapter deals with the findings and suggestions which have been deduced on the basis of analysis and interpretations of data collected and reported in connection with this research project. The matter presented in this chapter has been divided mainly in four parts. Part A deals with the answers to hypotheses presented in chapter I, part B reports the main findings followed by generalizations and conclusions, part C deals with some suggestions and part D presents some problems for further research.

PART A

ANSWERS TO HYPOTHESIS

Hypothesis No. 1

(Ho) "The performance of the girls residing with working mothers and non-working mothers is the same on different motivational variables under study".

(Hi) "The performance of the girls residing with working mothers and non-working mothers is unequal on different motivational variables under study".

In this connection the study reports as follows :

(1) At age 9 and 11 the performance of the girls residing with the working mothers and non-working mothers on achievement motivation has been found to be the same. But it significantly differs among the two groups at age 13. At this stage the level of achievement motivation is significantly high among the girls residing with the non-working mothers.

(2) At all the three stages of development the level of manifest anxiety is the same among both the groups of girls.

(3) At age 9 and 11 the girls residing with working mothers and non-working mothers have displayed same level of self concept but at age 13 the girls residing with the non-working mothers have reported a significantly well developed self concept as compared to the girls residing with the working mothers.

(4) At age 9 and 11 the girls residing with the working mothers and the girls residing with the non-working mothers has displayed same level of intellectual maturity but at age 13 the girls residing with the non-working mothers have displayed a higher level of intellectual maturity.

(5) At all the three age levels the level of emotional maturity have been found more or less the same among both the groups of girls.

(6) At all the three age levels the level of social maturity has also been found to be the same among the girls residing with the working mothers and non-working mothers.

Hypothesis No. 2

(Ho) "The performance of the girls residing with working mothers and non-working mothers is the same on different personality variables under study".

(Hi) "The performance of the girls residing with working mothers and non-working mothers is unequal on different personality variables under study".

In this connection the study reports as follows:-

I Personality Factors :

(1) On factors A,B,C, and D, of Children's Personality Questionnaire (CPQ) the performance of the girls residing with the working mothers and the performance of the girls residing with non-working mothers shows no significant differences and is practically the same at all the three levels or stages.

(2) On factor E, at age 9 the girls residing with the non-working mothers are significantly more obedient. At age 11 and 13 the performance of the girls is practically the same on factor E.

(3) On factor F, at age 9 and 11 the girls residing with the working mothers have displayed a trend towards enthusiasm. At age 13 both the groups on factor F stand more or less at the equal level.

(4) On factor G, the performance of the girls residing with the working and non-working mothers is the same at all the three age levels.

(5) On factor H, at age 9 the girls residing with the working mothers have been found comparatively more venturesome than the girls residing with non-working mothers. But at 11 and 13 the performance of both the groups on this factor is the same.

(6) On factor I, J, N and O, the performance of the girls residing with the working and non-working mothers is practically the same at all the stages or age levels.

(7) On factor Q3, at age 9 and 11 the performance of the girls residing with the working and non-working mothers is the same but at age 13 the girls residing with the non-working mothers are significantly more controlled than the girls residing with the working mothers.

(8) On factor Q4, at age 9 and 11 both the groups of girls stand with no significant difference, rather at the same level. At age 13 the girls residing with the non-working mothers are comparatively more relaxed, and the girls residing with the working mothers are less relaxed.

II Reactions to Frustrations:

(1) On obstacls dominance (OD), at age 9 and 11 the girls residing with working and non-working mothers have not shown any significant difference in their performance but at age 13, the girls residing with the working mothers have comparatively displayed more obstacle dominance.

(2) On Ego defence (ED), at age 9 and 11 the performance of the girls residing with working and non-working mothers is more or less the same. At age 13 the girls residing with the non-working mothers have comparatively reported better and stronger ego defence than the girls residing with the working mothers.

(3) On need persistance (NP), the performance of the girls residing with the working and non-working mothers is more or less the same.

(4) On Exprapunitiveness, at age 9 and 11 the performance of the girls residing with the working and non-working mothers is more or less the same. But at age 13, the girls residing with the working mothers have displayed more of extrapunitiveness as compared to the girls residing with non-working mothers.

(5) On Intropunitiveness, the performance of the girls residing with the working and non-working mothers is the same at all the three age levels.

(6) On impunitiveness at age 9 and 11, the performance of the girls residing with the working and non-working mothers is the same. But at age 13, the girls residing with the non-working mothers have displayed more of impunitiveness than the girls residing with working mothers.

Hypothesis No. 3

(Ho) "The onset of puberty does not bring about significant differences in the performance of girls on different variables under study".

(Hi) "The onset of puberty brings about significant differences in the performance of girls on different variables under study".

In this connection the study reports as follows:-

Motivational Variables:

(1) The level of achievement motivation has not significantly gone up among girls with working mothers with the onset of puberty, but it has improved among girls with non-working mothers. At the pubertal stage the girls with non-working mothers have displayed higher achievement motivation.

(2) With the onset of puberty, the level of manifest anxiety in both the groups of girls has gone up.

(3) The self concept of the girls with working mothers has not significantly changed with the onset of puberty, but it has improved among girls with non-working mothers.

(4) With the onset of puberty, the level of intellectual maturity has gone down among girls with working mothers, but not among girls with non-working mothers. The pubertal age group with non-working mothers has displayed significantly high intellectual maturity.

(5) The Emotional maturity among girls with working mothers has shown a significant decrease with onset of puberty, but not so in the case of girls with non-working mothers.

(6) The level of social maturity among both the groups of girls has been found to be the same even at the onset of puberty.

Personality variables:

(7) The performance of both the groups of girls have not shown significant differences with the onset of puberty on factors A, B, C, D, G & N.

(8) On factor E, the performance of girls with working mothers has changed with the onset of puberty, but not in the case of girls with non-working mothers.

(9) On factor F, the performance of both the groups of girls has changed with the onset puberty in the same direction.

(10) On factor H, the performance of girls with working mothers has changed with the onset of puberty, but not in case of the girls with non-working mothers.

(11) On factor I, the performance of both the groups of girls has changed with the onset of puberty, and in the same direction.

(12) On factor J, the performance of both the groups of girls has significantly changed with the onset of puberty.

(13) On factor O, the performance of both the groups of girls has changed significantly with the onset of puberty.

(14) On factor Q3, the performance of girls with working mothers has changed with the onset of puberty, but not in case of girls with non-working mothers.

(15) On factor Q4, the performance of girls with working mothers has changed with the onset of puberty, but not in case of non-working mothers.

Reactions to Frustration:

(16) With the onset of puberty, the girls with working mothers have displayed higher obstacle dominance, but its level has not changed among girls with non-working mothers.

(17) With the onset of puberty,the Ego defence has weakened among girls with working mothers, but it has remained static among girls with non-working mothers . The pubertal age group of girls with non-working mothers has displayed high Ego defence.

(18) With the onset of puberty, the need persistance among girls of both the groups has increased, more or less equally and significantly.

(19) With the onset of puberty, the tendency of Extrapunitiveness has come down among both the group of girls.

(20) With the onset of puberty, the tendency of Intropunitiveness has risen among both the groups of girls quite significantly.

(21) With the onset of puberty, the tendency of impunitiveness has also gone up among both the groups of girls.

PART B

MAIN FINDINGS

MOTIVATIONAL VARIABLES

Achievement Motivation

At the prepubertal stages the level of achievement motivation, as displayed by the girls residing with the working mothers and by the girls residing with the non-working mothers has been very close to each other. But with the entry into pubertal stage,the level of achievement motivation among the girls residing with non-working mothers has shown a significant upward trend. Comparatively the girls residing with the working mothers have not shown any upward trend. At the pubertal stage the girls residing with the non-working mothers have displayed higher level of achievement-motivation as compared to those residing with the working mothers.

The grouping of girls on the basis of mother's professions have reported significantly high achievement motivation among the girls whose mothers are employed in the medical and teaching professions and are doing office jobs. The girls with mothers self employed have displayed low level of achievement motivation.

Manifest Anxiety

At the prepubertal stages both the groups of the girls residing with the working mothers and residing with the non- working mothers have manifested practically same level of anxiety. At the further stages of development, a significant increase and rise in anxiety has been noted among both the groups of girls. The onset of puberty reports in both the groups, high level of anxiety as compared to the earlier stages of development. The comparison of the girls grouped on the basis of mother's professions discloses that the level of anxiety among all the groups is practically the same irrespective of the fact what is the profession of the working mothers.

Self Concept

The self concept as reported by the girls residing with the working mothers, and the girls residing with the non-working mothers at the prepubertal stage is of the same stature. Somehow, the situation has been found a bit different at the further stages of development. The position of self concept among the girls residing with the working mothers practically remains to be the same upto the pubertal age. The self concept has quite significantly improved continiously at the further stages of development among the girls residing with the non-working mothers. At the pubertal stage, the self concept as reported by the girls of the non-working mothers is comparatively much more developed. The groupwise comparisons based on mothers professions report no significant differences in the self concept, as developed by the various groups of girls.

MATURITY

a. Intellectual Maturity

At the prepubertal stage, both the groups of girls have displayed more or less the same level of intellectual maturity. But at the further stages of development, a marked difference is noted among both the groups. The girls with the working mothers have shown a significant downward trend in intellectual maturity upto the pubertal stage. On the other hand, the level of intellectual maturity among girls residing with non-working mothers remains to be the same throughout the development process. At the pubertal stage, the level of intellectual maturity among girls with non-working mothers is significantly higher than those who reside with the working mothers.

Among the girls grouped on the basis of mothers professions, the girls who are residing with the mothers self employed or engaged in teaching and medical professions have shown a sound level of intellectual maturity. But however the girls residing with the mothers engaged in office jobs have reported low level of intellectual maturity.

b. Emotional Maturity

At the prepubertal stage, the girls of both the groups have more or less exhibited emotional maturity at the same level, but the situations have changed significantly with the entry of groups of girls into the pubertal stage. The girls residing with the working mothers have shown a significant decrease in the emotional maturity, whereas the girls residing with the non- working mothers have maintained the same level of emotional maturity at the pubertal stage. In other words, the girls with non-working mothers have retained their previous level of emotional maturity.

The comparison of the girls grouped on the basis of mothers professions discloses that the girls residing with the mothers self employed and engaged in teaching professions have exhibited better emotional maturity, as compared to the girls whose mothers are engaged in office jobs. Somehow the level of emotional maturity among the girls residing with the mothers engaged in medical professions is not very low.

c. Social Maturity

Both the groups of girls have displayed the same level of social maturity at the prepubertal stage. At the further stages of development both the groups of girls have displayed and maintained that level. At the pubertal stage too, the level of social maturity among both the groups of girls is more or less the same. The comparison of the girls grouped on the basis of mothers professions also do not disclose anything. Practically all the four groups of girls, irrespective of their mothers professions, have displayed the same level of social maturity.

PERSONALITY VARIABLES

PERSONALITY FACTORS

Factor A - Reserved vs Warmhearted

The performances of the girls residing with the working mothers and the girls residing with the non-working mothers have not differed significantly right from the prepubertal stage to the pubertal stage of development. It is clear that both the groups of girls at all levels of development have exhibited warm heartedness more or less equally. Among the girls grouped on the basis of mother's profession, the girls residing with the mothers self employed have comparatively exhibited more warm heartedness than those girls whose mothers go out, on office jobs or are engaged in medical and teaching professions.

Factor B - Dull vs Bright

On this factor also both the groups of girls have exhibited same level of intelligence right from the prepubertal stage to pubertal stage. The agewise differences among both the groups of girls have not been reported. The study of girls grouped on the basis of mothers profession tells that the intellectual display among the four groups of girls is the same irrespective of the fact which profession have been chosen by the mothers.

Factor C - Affected by feelings vs Emotionally stable

On this factor, both the groups of girls have shown same type of development right from the stage of prepuberty to the stage of puberty. The agewise comparisons among both the groups of girls also show that the performance of both the groups of girls is practically the same on this factor. The trend of scores among both the groups of girls discloses that the girls residing with the working mothers and the girls residing with the non- working mothers are emotionally stable equally, even at the pubertal stage. The groupwise comparison among girls based on mothers professions of course reveal that the girls residing with the mothers self employed and engaged in medical professions are more stable.

Factor D - Phlegmatic vs Excitable

On this factor too the performance of both the groups of girls is practically the same right from the prepubertal stage to pubertal stage. The agewise comparisons also disclose that the possession of this trait among both the groups of girls is practically the same at all ages. The trend of scores on this factor helps to say that all the girls under both the situations are equally phlegmatic. The comparison of girls grouped on the basis of mothers professions also have reported that all the girls are equally phlegmatic, irrespective of the mothers professions.

Factor E - Obedient vs Dominant

On this factor, the girls residing with the non-working mothers have been found more obedient, mild and accomodating at the prepubertal stage as compared to the girls residing with the working mothers. Further, the development of both the groups of girls from prepubertal to pubertal stage is of the same nature. The agewise comparisons further report among both the groups of girls same nature or behaviour even at the pubertal stage. The comparisons of the girls grouped on the basis of the mothers professions tells that all the groups are equally obedient, mild and accomodating irrespective of their mothers professions.

Factor F - Sober vs Enthusiastic

The study on this factor has reported that at the prepubertal stage, the girls residing with the non-working mothers are comparatively more sober than the girls residing with the working mothers. At the further stages, the development among both the groups of girls is significant, but among the girls with working mothers is slightly more from soberity to enthusiasm. At the pubertal stage the difference is there but it is not significant. The comparison of girls grouped on to the basis of mothers professions have displayed that the girls residing with the mothers engaged in medical profession are more enthusiastic. The girls of all the other three groups are more or less, less enthusiastic and have displayed soberity.

Factor G - Expedient vs Conscientious

On this factor the performance of both the groups of girls right from the stage of prepuberty to the stage of puberty has been practically the same. The agewise difference are also not visible. The trend of scores has disclosed that practically all the girls in both the situations are equally conscientious and possess the mentality of following rules and regulations. The comparison of girls grouped on the basis of mothers professions has disclosed that the girls residing with the mothers doing office jobs are significantly less conscientious. On the other hand the girls residing with the mothers engaged in other three professions are more conscientious.

Factor H - Shy vs Venturesome

The study on this factor has disclosed that the girls residing with the working mothers are more venturesome, uninhibited and socially bold at the prepubertal stage, than those residing with the non-working mothers. Further, at the other stages of development these girls have shown a downward trend on this factor.On the other hand, the girls with non- working mothers have maintained the same level of performance and so they have remained equally venturesome at all the stages. At the pubertal stage the girls with working mothers have not been found so much venturesome and socially bold as they were in the beginning. The comparison of the girls grouped on the basis of mothers profession have shown that the girls residing with the mothers doing office jobs are practically less socially bold and inhibited, whereas the girls residing with the mothers engaged in other three professions have been found more socially bold and venturesome.

Factor I - Toughmindedness vs tendermindedness

At the prepubertal stage the girls of both the groups are equally tenderminded, but at the further stages of development up to that of puberty, a downward trend in scores have been noted among girls of both the groups upto the age of puberty. It seems that both the groups are moving towards toughmindedness. The display at all the stages of development is more or less the same among both the groups of girls. The comparison of girls grouped on the basis of mothers professions has disclosed that the girls residing with the self employed mothers and those engaged in teaching profession are more tenderminded than those whose mothers are self employed or engaged in medical profession.

Factor J - Zestful vs Circumspect Individualism

At the prepubertal stage both the groups of girls are equally vigorous and zestful. At the further stages of development right from the prepubertal to pubertal stage, both the groups have exhibited significant gain in scores. This has disclosed their movements towards cirumspect individualism which refers to their becoming internally restrained and reflective in attitude and behaviour. At all the stages of development however the performance of both the groups of girls is same. The comparison of the girls grouped on the basis of mothers professions has disclosed that the girls residing with the mothers self employed and engaged in medical and teaching professions are comparatively more vigorous, zestful and like group actions.

Factor N - Forthright vs Shrewd

On this factor practically both the groups of girls have exhibited forthright and natural behaviour at the prepubertal stage and also at all the further stages of development upto puberty. No agewise differences are noted. The comparison of the girls grouped on the basis of mothers professions also shows that all the groups of girls are equally natural and forthright in their behaviour irrespective of the fact which profession their mothers belong to.

Factor O - Self-Assured vs Guilt-Prone

On this factor both the groups of girls have shown significant development right from prepubertal stage to pubertal stage. However the trend has disclosed that inspite of this development at all the stages, both the groups of girls equally have a feeling of security and are equally self assured and confident. The comparison of the girls grouped on the basis of mothers profession has shown that all the four groups of girls are equally self assured and confident irrespective of the professions, their mothers have chosen.

Factor Q_3 - Undisciplined Self-Conflicts vs Controlled

On this factor both the groups of the girls have exhibited same level of performance at the prepubertal stage. In other words they are equally controlled, compulsive and socially precise. But at the further stages upto that of puberty the girls residing with the working mothers have shown a significant downward trend in scores and they have become less controlled. On the other hand the girls residing with non-working mothers are equally controlled at all the stages of development and so reflected stability in their behaviour. The result is that at the pubertal stage the girls with non-working mothers are more controlled whereas girls with working mothers are less controlled. The comparison of girls grouped on the basis of mothers professions shows that the girls residing with the mothers self employed, doing office jobs and engaged in teaching are comparatively more controlled than those whose mothers are engaged in medical profession.

Factor Q_4 - Relaxed vs Tense

At the prepubertal stage the girls of both the groups have been found equally relaxed, unfrustrated and composed. But at the further stages of development from prepubertal to pubertal stage, the girls residing with the working mothers have shown an upward trend in scores, meaning thereby that they have started to develop frustration, and becoming less composed. On the other hand, the girls residing with the non-working mothers have not moved in any direction even at the further stages of development. They maintained this trait at the same level. However, at the pubertal stage the girls with non-working mothers are more relaxed and unfrustrated as compared to those residing with working mothers. The comparison of girls grouped on the basis of mothers professions has shown that the girls residing with mothers self employed and with mothers engaged in teaching professions are comparatively more relaxed and unfrustrated.

REACTION TO FRUSTRATION

Obstacle Dominance (OD)

At the prepubertal stage, both the groups of girls have displayed obstacle dominance practically at the equal level. But at the further stages of development the obstacle dominance among girls residing with the working mothers has significantly increased from prepubertal to pubertal stage. Whereas the level of obstacle dominance has remained practically the same among the girls with non-working mothers at all these stages of development. Comparatively the obstacle dominance has been exhibited significantly at a higher level by the girls residing with the working mothers at the pubertal stage, than the girls residing with the non-working mothers. The comparison of the girls grouped on the basis of mothers professions has disclosed that the girls residing with the mothers self employed and doing office jobs have exhibited significantly higher obstacle dominance as compared to the girls whose mothers are engaged in medical and teaching professions.

Ego Defence (ED)

Among both the groups of girls the level of Ego defence is practically the same at the prepubertal stage. At the further stages of development upto the pubertal stage, the level of Ego defence significantly comes down which shows that at the pubertal stage, the girls residing with the working mothers have exhibited weak Ego defence. The level of Ego defence remains more or less the same at all the stages of development among girls residing with the non-working mothers. At the pubertal stage, the study has disclosed that the girls residing with the non-working mothers have exhibited stroger Ego defence as compared to the girls residing with the working mothers. The comparison of girls grouped on the basis of mothers professions has reported that the girls residing with the mothers self employed and engaged in teaching and medical professions have displayed strong Ego defence, when on the other hand the girls residing with the mothers doing office jobs have displayed weak ego defence.

Need Persistance (NP)

At the prepubertal stage both the groups of girls have exhibited Need Persistance more or less at the same level. But at the further stages of development, the need persistance has significantly increased among the girls residing with the working mothers. The increase of need persistance has also been reported by the girls residing with non-working mothers at the earlier stages of development, but not appreciably. The agewise comparisons show that at all age levels need persistance is more or less equally present among both the groups of girls. The comparison of the girls grouped on the basis of mothers professions shows that the need persistance is comparatively high among girls whose mothers are engaged in teaching and medical professions, and doing office jobs. Somehow comparatively, it is low among girls whose mothers are self employed.

Extrapunitiveness (E)

The tendency of extrapunitiveness has been exhibited at the equal level practically by the girls of both the groups at the prepubertal stage. At the further stages from prepubertal to pubertal, the tendency of extrapunitiveness or throwing blame on others in the environment significantly comes down in both the groups of girls. Still at the pubertal stage this tendency is highly present among the girls residing with the working mothers as compared to the girls residing with the non-working mothers. The comparison of the girls grouped on the basis of mothers professions reports that among all the groups the tendency of extrapunitiveness is more or less equally present irrespective of the fact which profession their mothers belong to.

Intropunitiveness (I)

At the prepubertal stage, the tendency of intropunitiveness has been reported practically at the same level by both the groups of girls. At the further stages of development the tendency of intropunitiveness or accepting blame has increased significantly among both the groups of girls continuously upto the pubertal stage. This increase in both the groups is quite significant. But somehow, the agewise comparisons report that at all ages this tendency is more or less equally present among both the groups of girls. The comparison of the girls grouped on the basis of mothers professions shows that this tendency is equally present among all the groups of girls irrespective of the fact which profession has been chosen by their mothers.

Impunitiveness (M)

At the prepubertal stage, the tendency of impunitiveness or evading blame is equally present among both the groups of girls. At the further stages of development this tendency significantly has increased among both the groups of girls. But still the increase is more marked among the girls residing with the non- working mothers. At the pubertal stage, this tendency of impunitiveness or evading blame is significantly much high among the girls residing with the non-wrking mothers as compared to the girls residing with working mothers. The comparison of the girls grouped on the basis of mothers professions has reported that this tendency of impunitiveness is more or less equally present among all the groups of girls irrespective of the fact which profession has been chosen by their mothers.

Observations based on case study

The studies of individual cases and their interviews disclosed that in the case of girls residing with the working mothers achievement motivation comes from other sources and not from parents in most of the cases. The factors leading to anxiety and frustration are mostly absence of mother's guidance, unsolved personal problems, burdens of household chores, heavy courses of study and high expectations and unrealistic demands of parents. The lack of academic gudiance and discussions, side by side with too much interferences, tensions in the home environment and missing of social situations leads to immaturity among them in the emotional, intellectual and social areas. Moreover unrealistic goals, busy schedule of parents results in lack of communication with the parents leads to underprotection. Ultimately it results in the development of a weak personality. Somehow they feel that there are merits of mother's employment, for example economic uplift, status in society, development of self concept and strong ego, but still there are more of demerits for example, no discussion of family problems, poor training and guidance to children, poor hospitality to visitors and social relations and poor home adjustments.

On the other hand the girls residing with the non-working mothers have accepted in majority that achievement motivation comes first from parents. In majority they have presented few factors for anxiety and frustration and these are insufficient income, unfulfillment of needs and lack of recognition. They feel that lack of academic discussions, too much interference in studies, poor school achievement leads to immaturity. Poor development of personality and self concept, according to them is due to poor achievements in schools, lack of ego strength, unfulfilled ambitions side by side due to overprotection from parents which leaves no scope for exploration and adventures. For most of them the only merit of mother's employment is status in the society. The demerits according to them are poor hospitality to visitors, poor training of children and poor home adjustment.

GENERALIZATIONS

1. The girls residing with the working mothers have on the whole exhibited comparatively undeveloped self concept, deep developed anxiety and low levels of intellectual and emotional maturity. Social maturity and its development is rather static. This is the reason probably that they have exhibited poor achievement motivation.

   On the other hand, the girls residing with the non-working mothers have exhibited positive development of self concept. Though the development of social maturity is also not appreciable and rather static among them, yet intellectual and emotional maturity do not show downward trend. The development of the two is also static. The level of anxiety among these girls can be observed is low. This group has exhibited high achievement motivation.

2. The girls residing with the working mothers seem to be more enthusiastic and venturesome.They have exhibited movement towards circumspect individualism, and it seems that they are becoming internally restrained. They also seem to be apprehensive, less relaxed and less controlled.

   On the other hand the girls residing with the non-working mothers are more obedient, more controlled and more relaxed. Somehow they are less enthusiastic, shy and less venturesome, less apprehensive and much more obedient.

   On other traits under study, performance of both the groups of girls does not show any noticeable difference. The girls of both the groups are equally warm hearted, emotionally stable, phlegmatic, conscientious, forthright and natural in behaviour.

3. On the variable of Reactions to Frustration, the girls residing with the working mothers have exhibited comparatively more obstacle dominance and more of need persistance. On the other side, they have exhibited development of weak Ego and weak Super Ego strength. They have also shown a tendency of high Extrapunitiveness and low Impunitiveness.

   On the other hand, girls with the non-working mothers have exhibited strong Ego defence and low obstacle dominance and further low need persistance.

The tendency of Extrapunitiveness is low in the girls residing with the non-working mothers, whereas the tendency of Impunitiveness is high among them. The tendency of Intrapunitiveness or accepting blame is equally present among the girls of both the groups.

4. The comparisons of the girls grouped on the basis of mother's profession have disclosed as follows:

   (a) The girls residing with the mothers engaged in medical profession have exhibited good self concept, static level of anxiety and a sound level of achievement motivation. The social maturity is normally present and intellectual and emotional maturity is rather not upto the appreciable limit. On the other hand these girls are more enthusiastic, emotionally stable, venturesome and conscientious, but less tenderminded and less relaxed. The obstacle dominance is low among them. Ego defence and need persistance seem to be strong.

   (b) The girls residing with the mothers engaged in the teaching profession have exhibited normal development of anxiety and self concept but good achievement motivation and good intellectual and emotional maturity. Social maturity seems to be just normal. These girls are more conscientious, more venturesome, more tenderminded and more controlled. They have presented low obstacle dominance, but strong Ego defence. Somehow the level of need persistance is comparatively high among them.

   (c) The girls residing with the mothers doing office jobs have exhibited low level of emotional maturity, but normal social and intellectual maturity. The development of self concept and anxiety is also normal.The achievement motivation is quite high among these girls. These girls are more vigorous, but somehow less venturesome and less relaxed. Somehow they have exhibited high obstacle dominance but a weak ego defence and high need persistance.

   (d) The girls residing with the mothers self employed have comparatively exhibited good emotional and intellectual maturity and normal development of social maturity. The development of self concept and presence of anxiety is just normal. Comparatively, achievement motivation is low among these girls. On the other hand, they are more warm hearted, more conscientious, more venturesome, more tederminded, more emotionally stable and controlled. They are less relaxed and they have exhibited high obstacle dominance. The need persistance is low among these girls and development of ego is good with strong ego defence.

5. The study of individual cases have revealed that mothers employment ultimately leaves no source in the home situations for motivating students towards high achievement, on the other hand heavy courses of studies side by side with burden of household work, and high expectation of parents lead to anxity and frustrations. All this ultimately results in the development of waek ego, intellectual and emotional immaturity and poor self concept.

CONCLUSION

The fact which ultimately instigated the investigator to pursue this research work was to locate and identify which of the variables under study are affected significanly and more in either directions by the maternal employment. This research has disclosed that, as compared to the girls residing with non- working mothers, the girls residing with the working mothers have reported low achievement-motivation, poorly developed self concept and low level of intellectual and emotional maturity. In addition to this, they have been found less obedient, internally restrained, less controlled, undergoing self conflict and tense. Among the reactions to frustrations, they have displayed more of obstacle dominance, more of need persistance and comparatively a weak ego defence, side by side with this, they have also displayed more of extrapunitiveness.

But when an attempt is made to elicit facts on the positive side, it is noted that, comparatively, the girls residing with the working mothers are more dominant, possesing leadership qualities, more enthusiastic and venturesome, vigorous, forthright and self assured. Of course, they have displayed more of extrapunitiveness, obstacle dominance and low impunitiveness. But it should be accepted that these are the personality variables which can be displayed more only by those who are quite intelligent and shrewd. So all these can be exploited for the better ends. The investigator earnestly feels that with advancements in science and technology, and in the interest of national reconstruction and development, specially when world organizations are attempting to utilize the talents and energies of women in various directions, in INDIA one can not afford to leave mothers at home simply to care and look after the child. Again psychological researches have shown that certain specific ablities are comparatively found more among the females. These are verbal ability, space relations ability, memory and perceptual ability. Still, girls have been found doing well on jobs related to mechanical ability, numerical ability and reasoning ability. Today there are countries which have started realizing that jobs, which are related to such abilities where girls excel, should be given to ladies first. Under such circumstances, how can we think of asking the women to stay at home and to look after the household needs and care of children.

The investigator here earnestly feels that working mothers should plan their activities with utmost care and responsibility, having full co-operation of their husbands, in a way that their children may receive proper achievement motivation with a minimum of anxiety and frustration. It is their duty to see that their children develop correct self concept and well balanced personality. If activities are planned properly and wisely, even within home situations, the children can develop as a good mature individuals having strong Ego and superego.

To help in this direction some suggestions follow:

PART C

SUGGESTIONS

1. The first and foremost suggestion is for the parents under conditions where both the parents go on jobs. It is suggested that both the parents should draw a well planned day's schedule in which they should steal few hours to look after the needs of the children. This is more necessary in the case of girls because here significant differences have been found more at the pubertal stage. It would be much better if parents can also look for the academic needs, because it will provide indirectly better achievement motivation to children and minimize frustration. The atmosphere should be full of affection, healthy and permissive. This is necessary because such atmosphere is free of tensions, provides security to children, and develops strong Ego with self confidence.

2. The parents should attempt to gain full confidence of the teachers from schools to know the strengths and weaknesses of their sons and daughters with a view to improve the situation through self efforts. It should be noticed here that, where conditions allow, both sons and daughters can be easily handled and guided even for the academic improvements by the mothers. Aggression should not be allowed to enter at any phase even when sons or daughters committ mistakes.

3. Where mothers work, naturally the economic conditions are likely to improve. Under such situations, there should be sufficient provision for books etc., and other such necessities to allow full motivation for achievement. All possible help should be given in home work and during study hours children should not be disturbed. The household chores can be shared by both the parents. This will allow mothers a psychological well being.

4. Where possible, children can be subjected for educational and vocational guidance through proper testing with the help of career masters and guidance workers in schools or through district psychologists to have a full account of the intellectual abilities and personality factors. This will help the parents to

develop correct self concept among children. Here, a caution is to be taken - 'No criticisms' for the weaknesses. On the other hand, both parents and children should accept the realities. This ultimately leads to "No frustrations".

5. The personal problems of the children should be discussed from time to time and a solution to these should be searched out. Children should be encouraged to solve their own problems as for as possible. In the case of girls, mothers have to take a lead. This will develop self confidence among children.
6. The parents should not set unrealistic goals for their children and should not have high expectations. All these things should be set after taking into account the abilities of children, their strengths and limitations.
7. To develop proper intellectual maturity, discussions from time to time in free hours can be taken up on academic topics, political and social problems in healthy atmosphere. Discussions should be friendly. On problems of personal nature, mothers can guide daughters individually.
8. To develop proper emotional maturity, the negative emotions like fear, anger jealousy, hatred etc. should not be allowed to enter in home atmosphere. Mothers here can guide their daughters well, and both the parents can guide their sons well. To have a better control of the negative emotions, the discussion on personal problems related with jobs should not be allowed to spoil the home atmosphere.
9. There is an example in history where Nelson said "I won the battle of waterloo on the field of Eton".The public schools strongly believe that games, sports and indoor games develop best qualities for better personality development. Here, both the parents can take up discussions on national sports and games from time to time. In home environment, indoor games can be taken up for a good passtime where all should participate irrespective of age. This develops a permissive atmosphere.
10. The parents must find out time for social visits and should not miss, as for as possible, programmes in towns and social gatherings. Where necessary, girls should accompany their mothers. Exhibitions should never be missed. All this develops

intellectual as well as social maturity and sometimes even social skills. At times, this also helps in achievement motivation and sometimes both sons and daughters set their own hobbies or lines for achieving certain roles.

11. It is an age of competitions. Children are often asked to compete by the different organizations through participation in exhibitions, games, sports, literary ares, paintings, dance and music programmes and such others. Here, every encouragement should be given by both the parents to their sons and daughters. This develops good personal qualities and confidence.

12. Both overprotection and underprotection cause and lead to anxiety and frustration. To avoid this both sons and daughters should be trained specially by the working mothers to take up responsibilities independently, specially, where both the parents are attending jobs. This will provide good training for future. But to avoid underprotection, a kean eye, observation and supervision is needed.

There is every possibility for more suggestions. The investigator feels that a lot will be attained if both the working parents take up some of the above mentioned suggestions seriously. This may develop a better atmosphere in home situation and in the faimly, ultimately leading to better development of personality among children.

PART D

SUGGESTIONS FOR FURTHER RESEARCH

1. It is suggested that a study of the attitudes of both boys and girls residing with the working mothers should be made in detail. This must include attitude towards father, attitude towards mother, attitude towards siblings, attitude towards visitors, attitude towards teachers and attitude towards classmates. In addition to this, attitude towards studies, attitude towards household work, and attitude towards the family in general should be included. Here comparisons can be made with the attitudes of boys and girls residing with the non-working mothers.
2. The direction of aggression can be studied in detail. Further details related to extrapunitiveness, intropunitiveness and impunitiveness can be studied. A comparison here also will be of much advantage.
3. Due to maternal employment some conditions encourage various types of projections. Here a detailed study of the defence mechanisms, adopted under such conditions by the boys and girls residing with the working mothers, can disclose much.
4. This research study can be repeated as such on boys also.
5. A longitudinal study on both boys and girls on all these variables of study can also be fruitful. Here the sample should be limited according to the conditions of study.

BIBLIOGRAPHY

BOOKS

– Aggarwal, J.C. (1966). *Educational Research - An Introduction.* New Delhi: Man Singh Arya Book Depot.

– Ambron, S.R. (1975). *Child Development.* Sanfrancisco: Rinehart Press.

– American Psychological Association. (1983) *Publication manual* (3rd ed.). Washington, DC: Author.

– Anand, Suchitra, Ramanirao, S.V. and Kapoor, Kavita (eds). (1986) *Women at work in India* - A Bibliography (Institute of Social Studies Trust). New Delhi: Sage Publication.

– Anderson, J. Durston, B.H. and Poole, M. (1970). *Thesis And Assignment Writing.* Sydney. John Wiley and Sons Australasia Pvt. Ltd.

– Anne, Marie Amber (1992). The effect of children on parents. New York: Haworth Press.

– Baik, Indira and Ratna, Malika. *Problems of working mothers* in Rajasthan Patrika. 15 August, 1977.

– Barr, Wesley R. (1979) *Contemporary theories about the family.* (Vol. I). New York: Free Press.

– Bernhart, K.B. (1964). *Discipline and child guidance.* New York: Mc Graw Hill.

– Berk, Lara E. (1989). *Child development.* London: Allyn and bacon Publisher.

– Best, J.W. and Kahn J.V. (1986). *Research in Education* (5th ed.). New Delhi: Prentice Hall of India Ltd

– Bhattacharya, S. (1985). *Psychology of child development.* New Delhi: Sterling Pulishers Pvt. Ltd.

– Bischof, Lodford J. (1970). *Interpreting personality theories* (2nd ed.). London: Harper and Row Publishers.

– Boring, E.G. (1963). *Foundations of psychology.* New Delhi: Asia Publishing House.

– Brisbane, H.E. (1965). *The Developing Child.* Peoria: C.A. Benett.

– Brophy, J.E. (1977). *Child development and socialization.* Chicago: Science Research Associates Inc.

– Buch, M.B. (Ed.). (1983). *A Survey of Research in Education.* Baroda: Centre of Advanced Study in Education.

– Charterl, J.J. (1978). *Child development and personality.* (5th ed.). New York: Harper and Row.

– Chauhan, S.S. (1983). *Psychology of Adolescence.* Bombay: Allied Pacific Pvt. Ltd.

- Chowdhary, P.K. (1987).*Changing values among young women.*New Delhi: Amar Prakashan.
- Cole, Luella (1965).*Psychology of Adolescence.* New York: Holt, Rinehart and Winston. Inc.
- Craig, G.J. (1979). *Child development.* Englewood Cliffs. N.J: prentice-H from ten to sixteen. London: Hamish Hamilton.
- Crow, L.D. and Crow, A. (1965).*Adolescent Development and Adjustment.* New York: Mc Graw Hill.
- Crow, L.D. and Crow, A. (1966).*Being a good parent.* Boston: Cristopher Publishing Company.
- Dinkmeyer, D.C. (1965). *Child development; the emerging self.* Englewood Cliffs NJ: Prentice-Hall.
- Dorothywood. (1960). *Test Construction.* Columbus, Ohio: Charles E. Merril.
- Evans, E.D. and Candles, B.M. (1978).*Children and youth Psycho-Social development* (2nd Ed.). New York: Holt Rinehart and Winston Inc.
- Featheringill, E.S. (1965).*How to be a successful Mother*New York: Morrow Publishing Company.
- Feinstein, K.W. (Ed.). (1979).*Working Women and Families.* Sage year Books in Women's Policy Studies.
- Gardner, D.B. (1964).*Development in early childhood.* New York: Harper and Row.
- Garrett, H.E. (1985).*Statistics in Psychology and Education.* Bombay: Vakils, Feffer and Simon's Private Ltd.
- Gessell, A., Ilg, F.L. and Ames, L.B. (1956).*Youth The years from ten to sixteen.* London : Hamish Hamilton.
- Goddard, C.L. (1962).*Child and his nurture.* Nashville: Abington Press.
- Goodrich, F.N. (1966).*Manual for expectant parents.* New Jersey: Prentice Hall.
- Goods, J.W. and Paul, K.H. (1952).*Methods in social research.* Tokyo: Tosho Printing Co. Ltd.
- Goods, W.J. (1989). *The Family*(2nd Ed.). New Delhi: Prentice Hall of India Pvt. Ltd.
- Gottfried, A.E. and Gottfried, A.W. (Eds). (1988).*Maternal employment and children's development.* New York: Plenum Press.
- *Guide to Indian Periodical Literature; Social Science and Humanities.* Haryana India: Indian Documentation Service Gurgaon.
- Gupta, K. (1983).*A Study of frustration among working women in relation to their needs, level of aspiration and some background variables.*Unpublished Ph.D. Thesis NASSDOC.
- Handerson, R.W. and Bergan, J.R. (1976).*The cultural context of childhood.* Coluembus Ohio: Charles E. Merrill Publishing Company.
- Hate, C.A. (1969).*Changing status of Indian women in post independent India.* Bombay: Allied Publishers Ltd.
- Hetherington, E.M. and Parke, R.D. (1986).*Child Psychology - A Contemporary view point* (3rd Ed.). New York: Mc Graw Hill Book Company.
- Hoffman, L.W. and Nye, F.L. (1974). *Working mothers.* San Francisco: Jossey-Bass.
- Hurlock, Elizabeth B. (1978).*Child development*(6th Ed.). New Delhi: Mc Graw-Hill International Book Company.
- Hurlock, E.B. (1982).*Developmental Psychology.* New Delhi: Tata Mc Graw Hill.

- Hurlock, Elizabeth B. (1976). *Personality development.* New Delhi: Tata Mc Graw-Hill Publishing Company Ltd.
- Indian Press Index, Delhi Library Assciation (PB 1270). Hardinge Public Library, Queen Garden.
- Index to Indian Periodicals Sociology and Psychology; National Social Science Documantation Centre, ICSSR, New Delhi.
- Jain, V.K. (Ed.). *Guide to Indian Periodical Literature.* Haryana: Prabhu Book Service, Gurgaon.
- Joyce, Wolfgang and Williams. (1980).*Middle childhood behaviour and development.* New York: Mac Millan Publishing Company Inc.
- Kapoor, Promila. (1982).*Conflict Between Adolescent Girls and Parents in India*New Delhi: Vision Books.
- Khare, P.N. (1979). *A Study of the Family life of Women earners of Indore City.* Unpublished Ph.D. Thesis.
- Kaul, Lokesh. (1984). *Methodology of Educational research.* New Delhi: Vikas Publishing Company.
- Kuhlen, R.G. (1982).*The Psychology of adolescent develop- ment.* New York: Harper and Brother.
- Kumari Pratima. (1988). *Changing values among young women.* New Delhi: Amar Prakashan.
- Kundu, C.L. (1977).*Personality development - A critique of Indian studies.* New Delhi: Vishal Publication.
- Kuppuswami, B. (1983).*Elements of social psychology.* New Delhi Vikas Publishing House Pvt. Ltd.
- Kuppuswamy, B. (1980). *A textbook of child bihaviour and development.* Ghaziabad: Vikas Publishing House.
- Liebero, R.B. and Spielger, M.D. (1987). *Personality strategies and issues*Chicago: Dorsey Press.
- Mies, Maria. (1980).*Indian women and patriarchy - Conflict and dilemmas of students of working women.* New Delhi: Concept Publishing Company.
- Mitra, S.K. (1982).*Survey of research in Psychology.* New Delhi: ICSSR.
- Mussen, P.H. Conger, J.J.Kegon, J. and Huston, A.C. (1984).*Child development and personality* (6th Ed.). New York: Harper and Row Publishers.
- Mussen, P.H. (1970). *Handbook of research methods in child development.* New Delhi: Wiley Eastern Pvt. Ltd.
- Newman, B.M. and Newman, P.R. (1979). *An Introduction to the Psychology of Adolescence.* Georgetown: The Dorsey Press.
- Nisbet, J.P. and Entwistle, N.J. (1970). *Educational Research methods.* London: University of London Press.
- Okun, B.F. (1978).*Working with adults - Individual family and career development.* California: Brooks/Cole Publishing Company.
- Owen, Peter. (1972). *Women at work - Combining family and Career.* London: Free Press.
- Paplia, D.E.and Sallywendkos O.(1979).*The child's world- infancy through adolescence.* New York: Mc Graw-Hill Book Company.
- Rani, Kala. (1976). *Role conflict in working women.* Delhi: Chetna Publications.
- Rao, Hanumantha. (1986). *The employed wife-mother: a study of the level of participation in housework, sex role orientations and companionship in marriage of*

working women in Tirupati. Unpublished doctoral thesis, Shri Venkateshwara University. Tirupati.

– Rauthus, S.A. and Nevid, J.S. (1980).*Adjustment and growth- The challenges of life.* New York: Rinehart and Winston Inc.

– *Readings in child development.* (1975). New York: Harcourt Brace and world.

– Research centre for women studies.*Who is who in women's studies in India.* Bombay: S.N.D.T. Women's University.

– Rogers, Dorothy. (1985). *Adolescents and youth.* Englewood Cliffs. N.J: Prentice-Hall.

– Sharma, C.D. (Ed.). *Index india.* Jaipur: Rajasthan University Library.

– Shreve, Anita. (1984).*The working mothers as role model*In New York Times Magazines September 9, 1984.

– Shrinivasan, K. and Ogale, N. (1985).*Economic, Psychic Cost benefit analysis of gainful employment of educated married mothers outside home.* ICSSR Project Report.

– Siegal, S. (1956). *Non Parametric statistics for the behavioural sciences.* Kogakusha: Mc Graw-Hill.

– Silverman, R.E. (1985).*Psychology.* New Delhi: Prentice Hall.

– Singh, Pushpa. (1988).*Role conflict among working women.* Delhi: Janki Prakashan.

– Singh, R.*Developmental Psychology In India,* An Annotated bibliography. (Vol.2). New Delhi: Sage Publications.

– Sodhi, Paramjeet. (1971).*Comparative study of social behaviour of nine year old children of working and non-working mothers.* Ph.D. Thesis. Chandigarh: Punjab University.

– Spock, B. (1962).*Problems of parents.* Boston: Houghton Mifflin.

Stewart, A.C. and Friedman, Susan. (1987). *Child development:* Infancy through adolescence. New York: John Wiley and Sons.

– Talwar, Usha. (1984).*Social profile of working women.* Jodhpur: Jain Brothers.

– Thompson, G.G. (1965).*Child Psychology.* (2nd Ed.). Bombay: The Times of India Press.

– Tilly, L.A. and Scott, J.W. (1987).*Women Work and Family.* New York and London: Methuen Inc.

– Trese, L.J. (1982).*Parent and child.* New York: Sheed and Ward.

– Tuckman, W.H. (1984). *Methods of educational research.* New Delhi: Vani Publishing.

– Venkataramana H.L. (1985). *Maternal employment: effect to personality. self ideal disparity, parent-child interaction andguilt factors.* Unpublished doctoral thesis, Andhra University, Waltair.

– VogalBall, Roultedge and Paul, K. (Ed.). (1961)*A Modern introduction to the family.* London: London Press.

– Warshal, S. and Goethal, G.E. (1979). *Adjustment path way to personal growth.* Englewood Cliffs. New Jersey: Prentice Hall Inc.

– Watson, R.I. and Lindgren, H.C. (1979).*Psychology of the child and the adolescents.* New York: Mac Millan Publishing Company.

– Winston, R. and Jolt (1980).*An Introduction to the principles of Psychology.* New York: Mc Graw-Hill.

– Wolfgang, W.J. (1980).*Middle childhood behaviour and development.* New York: Mac Millan Publishing Company.

– *Work and Family strategies in Asia.* Family researches in India: A review. Reports on two workshop published by C.W.D.S. Delhi.

JOURNALS

- American Journal of Orthopsychiatry. The American Association of Psychiatry. New York.
- American Psychologist. The American Psychological Association. Inc./400. North Uhle Street Arlington V.A.
- Asian Journal of Psychology and Education. Agra Psychological Research Cell (APRC). Tiwari Kothi. Belanganj.
- British Journal of Educational Psychology. British Psychological Society. St. Andrews House. 48 Princess Road. East Leicester L.E.
- California Journal of Educational Research: Department of Psychology: San Jose State University. San Jose: California.
- Child Development Abstracts and bibliography: The University of Chicago Press for the Society of Research in Child Development.
- Child Development. Chicago: University of Chicago Press for Society for Research in Child Development.
- Child Psychiatry Quarterly. Community Mental Health Centre. (Indra Health Home) Road 7. Banzara Hills. Hyderabad.
- Child Psychology Quarterly. Community Mental Health Centre. Delhi.
- Developmental Psychology. American Psychological Associa- tion. Inc. 1400 North Uhle Street Arlington V.A.
- Educational Research Quarterly. U.Sc. School of california for Education. Phillips Halt. Univ. Park Los Angles.
- Home Economocs Research Journal. American Home Economics Association. Sage Periodicals Press.
- ICSSR Journal of Abstracts and Reviews: Sociology, Social Anthropology, Criminology and Social Work. Delhi.
- Indian Dissertation Abstracts, Indian Council of Social Science Research. Association of Indian Universities. New Delhi.
- Indian Educational Review: A Research Journal. National Council of Educational Research and Training. New Delhi.
- Indian Journal of Current Psychological Research. Meerut: Dept. of Psychology. Institute of Advance Studies. Meerut University.
- Indian Journal of Home Science. Official Journal of Home Science Association of India. Coimbatore.
- Indian Journal of Personality and Human Development. CWDS. Delhi
- Indian Journal of Psychology and Education. Published by Indian Psychometric and Education Research Association. Patna.
- Indian Journal of Psychology. Indian Psychological Associa- tion. Calcutta University. College od Science. 92 Prafulla Chandra Road.
- Indian Psychological Abstracts: Quarterly published by Indian Council of Social Science Research. Ahmedabad.
- Indian Psychological Abstracts. Behavioural Science Centre. New Delhi: 32 Subhash Marg.
- International Journal of Psychology. International Union of Psychological Science. Lawrance Erlbaum Associates Ltd. 27 Palmeria Mensions. Church Road Hove. East Sussex.
- Journal of Child Psychology and Applied Disciplines: APA New York.

- Journal of Early Adolescence. 1201 Calla Elena. Juscon.
- Journal of Educational Psychology. American Psychological Association: Inc. Washington.
- Journal of Educational Research and Extension. Sri Ramakri- shna Mission Vidyalaya.
- Journal of Education and Psychology: Sardar Patel University. Vallabh Vidyanagar (India).
- Journal of Experimental Psychology, Learning, Memory and cognition, APA Arlington.
- Journal of Family Welfare : Family Planning Association of India, Bajaj Bhawan, Nariman Point Bombay.
- Journal of Genetic Psychology. American Psychological Association.
- Journal of Gujarat Research Society. Bombay. Samshodhan Sadan. Ramkrishna Mission Marg.
- Journal of Home Economics. American Home Economics Association Alexanderia.
- Journal of Institute of Education Research. Institute of Educa tional Research. Madras.
- Journal of Marriage and Family. National Council of Family Relations. Dept. of Sociology, Case Western Reserve University Cleveland Ohio.
- Journal of Marriage and Family Therapy. American Associan for marriage and Family Therapy Suite 407/1717 K Street New Washington.
- Journal of Personality and clinical studies. Delhi: Association of Clinical Psychology.
- Journal of Personality Assesment. Society for Personality Assesment. Lawrence Erlbaum Associates Publishers, Hillsdale New Jersey.
- Journal of Personality and Social Psychology, American Psychological Association. Inc. 1400 North Uhle Street Arlington.
- Journal of Psychological Researches. Madras : The Madras Psychology Society, Dept. of Psychology, University of madras.
- Journal of Youth and Adolescence. American Psychological Association.
- Population Review. Population Reference Bureau Inc. Washington. DC.
- Prachi Journal of Psycho-cultural dimensions. Meerut: Meerut University.
- Psychology and Aging. American psychological Association. Philadephia Geriatric Centre, 5301, Old York Road, Philadephia Pennsylvania.
- Psychological Bulletin and Psychological Review. American Psychological Association.
- Review of Educational Research. The University of Chicago Press. Chicago. The American Educational Research Associa- tion.
- Social Welfare. Central Social Welfare Board Samaj Kalyan Bhawan B-12, Taracrescant Institutional area South of IIT. New Delhi.
- The Indian Economic and Social History Review, Special number on survival, Politics and work: Indian women (1880- 1980) Delhi : Sage Publications India Ltd.
- The Council, Population Council Research Division, New York.
- University psychology Research Journal. University of Delhi.